THE PERSONAL NOTE

THE
PERSONAL NOTE
Or
FIRST AND LAST WORDS
FROM PREFACES, INTRODUCTIONS
DEDICATIONS, EPILOGUES

HERBERT J. C. GRIERSON
and
SANDYS WASON

Aedis Christi in Academia Oxoniensi
Olim Co-Alumni

What Horace says is

Eheu Fugaces
Anni labuntur, Postume, Postume !
Years glide away, and are lost to me, lost to me !
THOMAS INGOLDSBY

In my beginning is my end
T. S. ELIOT

1946

CHATTO & WINDUS
LONDON

PUBLISHED BY

Chatto & Windus

LONDON

*

Oxford University Press

TORONTO

Contents

CONTENTS

THE PERSONAL NOTE

AN INTRODUCTION
ON INTRODUCTIONS

BEING

A Preface to Prefaces

THE Preface or Introduction to a book is, I suppose, still in general skipped by at least more youthful readers.   It is later that a serious reader may discover that what is the first page of a book for the reader was the last for the author, and that a perusal of the preface may shed a light on the whole book that will obviate later misunderstandings, give the reader a glimpse of the writer's mind as he drew to a close, as he saw his own work in a final perspective—so much so that even the reader who has *not* neglected it at the outset may be tempted to turn back and re-read, and for him too the first words become the last.   This is not to say that all prefaces and introductions are important or interesting; not a few are more or less conventional acknowledgments of indebtedness and apologies for shortcomings.   Dr. Johnson, indeed, declared that there were two things he could do well—one was to describe what a book on a given subject should be, the other to explain why it had fallen short of the ideal outlined.   But some prefaces have a very definite interest of their own, and it is the quest of this which has directed our selection, and the consideration of this which is the motive of an Introduction on Introductions.

Three persons are combined in varying proportions in every author, and in every reader.   There is the person who is primarily interested in the subject-matter, his aim, if he be the composer, to present, if he be the reader, to apprehend, that as clearly and objectively as he can.   The great example of such composition is a mathematical proof; and that is the ideal of the student of science, the truth without concession to audience or self.   The degree to which the writer or reader succeeds in retaining this attitude depends very much on the nature of the subject, the field to which it belongs (compare, for example, mathematics and

I   B

theology), and the extent to which an objective and at the same time convincing presentation is obtainable. For in dealing with a great number, perhaps the majority, of subjects two other factors enter. To put it otherwise, there is in us another person who is acutely aware of his audience actual or prospective so far as the writer can forecast the latter. He is aware that he must make concessions in the way either of simplification or some recognition of existing prejudices. Finally, there is the person whose chief interest is in himself, his own sentiments and prejudices. The interest of some prefaces or dedications or epilogues is just to see personal feelings, which have been kept in check in the effort to be objective or conciliatory, break through, as if the author found relief in forgetting everything except his own convictions or hopes or fears. The expression of personal feeling is often blended with and may too easily be confounded with appeal to the feelings of the audience; for this is often more in appearance than reality. To take a very simple instance, the necessity of making a subject appear easy and attractive may to the author be inwardly a source of irritation, when to him it is perfectly clear without the simplification, which may involve some degree of falsification. The whole difference between oratory and poetry according to Keble and John Stuart Mill is just that the orator is primarily interested in awakening and directing the feelings of his audience, the poet in the adequate communication of his own.

But on occasions the most objective writer, the most intent on his theme, or again the most rhetorical, the most persuasive, will forget alike theme and audience and speak of himself. There could not well be a more impersonal, objective piece of work than a dictionary; yet Dr. Johnson could not keep his own prejudices out of some of his definitions, and when he came to write an introduction, a preface, he looks back in the most human way on his labours with touches alike of pathos and humour. The theme of Milton's great poem was more exalted, more sublime and superior to personal considerations, than the *Aeneid*. Yet the personal note breaks through in the preludes to three of the books. There was, or is, in organs and harmoniums, a stop which used to have a great attraction for me in childhood, the Vox Humana stop. It is the effect of that stop on my childish ear that I am reminded of when I read the first especially of these passages:

> *Thus with the year*
> *Seasons return, but not to me returns*
> *Day, or the sweet approach of Ev'n or Morn*, etc.,

and the same note, more pathetic if less exalted, is heard in the last verse of the unfinished *Faerie Queene* :

> *O that great Sabaoth God, graunt me that Sabaoths sight,*

and through the whole extent of the long preface to Raleigh's *Historie of the World*.

But the personal note in an introduction is not always, perhaps not often, so sombre; it does not suggest so much an entire absorption in oneself, if not to the forgetfulness of the other factors yet dominant throughout. Indeed, the interest of the introduction is just that the writer's consciousness of himself is always to some extent qualified by his consciousness of the other two factors. A reader might well say, "If you are in search of the personal note should you not go rather to a writer's private correspondence?" The fact is that we have purposely avoided letters, excepting one or two that are in the nature of public documents. To Charles Fox, a statesman, unknown to him personally, Wordsworth does not write quite as he would to Coleridge or might to Dorothy. There is, after all, a difference between what a man will say to a friend in confidence and what he will say when aware of a public audience, and of the particular relation to that audience in which his choice and treatment of a subject have placed him. In the former case he will say some things that he would be shy of saying in public, as for example Milton's confident declaration to his friend Diodati of the purity and elevation of his own aims. On the other hand he will utter at times what are passing thoughts, the humours and fancies of the moment. In a preface one will be more guarded, and in consequence it may be less, but also it may be more, sincere, more anxious to say only what one does really feel and will stand by if pressed. In a letter written when feeling a little lonely in the country, Wordsworth admits that "I wish much to be in town. Cataracts and mountains are good for occasional society, but they will not do for constant companions." On this Mr. Herbert Read somewhat solemnly pronounces that it amounts almost to a dissociation of personality. " It is a denial of the central doctrine of the *Prelude*, and one of those minute fissures of reality that make us doubt the autobiographical validity of that idealistic structure." I, too, am inclined to believe, with my old teacher, William Minto, that in the *Prelude* Wordsworth sees his past a little through the spectacles provided by the philosophical Coleridge. But surely in passing the above sentence upon Wordsworth Mr. Read attaches a little too much importance to the utterance of a fleeting, a very human, mood. We are human, social beings, and however sincerely we may enjoy being alone with Nature or our books, we long at times for moments when we may tell others how much we do enjoy the beauties of Nature and the company of books.

> *But grant me still a friend in my retreat*
> *Whom I may whisper, "Solitude is sweet."*

At least, if Wordsworth must be convicted of insincerity he will share the charge with Shelley, who in one letter writes to Peacock (April 30, 1818): "You may easily conjecture the motives which led us to forego the divine solitude of Como. To me, whose chief pleasure is the contemplation of nature, you may imagine how great is the loss." Yet in another letter to the same person, a little more than a year later (August 1819), he writes: "I most devoutly wish that I were living near London. . . . What are mountains, trees, heaths, or even the glorious and ever-beautiful sky, with such sunsets as I have seen at Hampstead, to friends? Social enjoyment, in some form or other, is the alpha and the omega of existence. All that I see in Italy—and from my tower window I now see the magnificent peaks of the Apennines half enclosing the plain—is nothing; it dwindles to smoke in the mind, when I think of some familiar forms of scenery, little perhaps in themselves, over which the old remembrances have thrown a delightful colour." Any reader of the letters of Byron and Shelley from Italy will soon discover that what they suffered from was intolerable boredom, the want of intellectual intercourse with those who could understand them, if it was Byron's weakness to prefer, as Scott says, "indifferent company rather than that of those whom he must, from character and talent, have necessarily conversed with most upon an equality." Both of them, in their different ways, sought relief in what company women could give them. Both of them welcomed with enthusiasm the advent of Trelawny and of Leigh Hunt.

In a preface, then, we have the interest of a complex reaction to the writer's own feelings, his awareness of his audience, and his subject.

To return to Milton: we have prefixed to the Preludes taken from the great poem a prose preface to the second book of the *Reason of Church Government* composed nearly twenty years earlier. A common thought or strain of consciousness runs through them both, the prose and the verse, but the tone, the temper, has changed markedly. The common thought is of himself as both prophet and poet, of the burthen laid on him, as on Jeremiah, making him "a man of strife and contention," but also the proud consciousness of his own gifts as a poet who "might perhaps leave something so written to after times as they would not willingly let it die." But the tone of the earlier preface is that of a young man with little or no experience of the world outside the domestic and the academic (and the same is true of the defence of his own conception of love and chastity in the *Apology of Smectymnuus*, which we might have cited). Before *Paradise Lost* was seriously taken in hand had come the sense of disillusionment. He was to write great poetry, epic and dramatic, but not quite in the tone of these joyous anticipations. His defence of love and chastity was sincere and deep, but alas! the later chapter in his *éducation sentimentale* was to include the pamphlets on freedom of divorce, and an at least theoretic justification of polygamy. The first of the three preludes is the most poignantly personal. Yet with the personal note is blended the consciousness of his great theme. His outward, physical blindness finds compensation in the inner spiritual vision of the Christian and the poet. In the second and third it is of his audience, a possibly critical or even hostile audience, that he becomes aware as well as of his theme: and there enters at once the touch of scorn (so recurrent in Milton's prose whether Latin or English) as he bethinks himself of the Court of Charles and the Restoration:

the barbarous dissonance
Of Bacchus and his revellers, etc.,

or contrasts his theme of universal human interest and significance with the older epics of wars or the later of jousts and feasts,

Not that which justly gives heroic name
To Person or to Poem.

But to Milton everything that concerned himself was of importance, and he lets us know also the contempt he has come to feel for Greek mythology—"an empty dream"—and his peculiar views about the influence of "an age too late or cold Climate" on poetry. If one talks about oneself, one runs the risk, unless protected by a sense of humour, of sliding into details which may disturb an impressive effect.

If we turn from Milton back to Chaucer we find him, too, aware of his audience, but in two very different moods. In the first he gives us a slyly humorous sketch of his appearance in the eyes of the host, and one may safely take the host's view as that of the majority of the company. "Who is this rather odd fellow, of no discoverable profession like the rest of us, and yet so observant?" —"a chiel's amang you takin' notes." And what is one to think of the recantation at the close of the *Tales*, its sweeping character? Chaucer is not built on the heroic lines of Milton. He is more human, under his occasional scepticism more superstitious. What one is reminded of is his own favourite Italian poet, Lollius, that is Boccaccio. Alarmed by a message from a Carthusian foretelling his early death, Boccaccio was seized by a similar access of fear and a desire "to destroy if he could the gay works of his youth, even the *Decameron*, and not only his poetry in the vulgar and his romances and stories, but the new learning itself, the study of antiquity, and to retire into a monastery" (*Giovanni Boccaccio*, by Edward Hutton: 1909). He was comforted and restored by Petrarch.

The nearest in intensity of feeling to the preludes of Milton is the preface to Raleigh's *Historie of the World*, from which we could make extracts only, but have tried to preserve this deep personal note. All his themes,—his personal suffering, "those inmost and soule-peircing wounds which are ever aking while uncured," the significance of history, *vanitas vanitatum*, the kind of audience he has to hope for or rather to fear, his treatment of them all is steeped in the same spirit and temper of pride and disillusionment.

It is of course the thought of his audience, his potential readers, that is the "first cause" of an introduction, of a preface being written at all, however much the other considerations may, as it goes on, predominate so as even to give to Milton's a touch of scorn for the audience. The degree to which the tone of an *apologia* will prevail depends on the consciousness of the author that he has to expect criticism or even opposition, that he is to some extent challenging the accepted views or the strong prejudices of his likely readers. The clearest examples here of such awareness of actual or possible hostility are the prefaces of Raleigh and Donne and the Dedication of Jonson's *Volpone*. Raleigh is too proud to make much attempt to conciliate the mass of readers: *unus mihi pro populo erat*. But Jonson's *Dedication* and Donne's Preface to his *Biathanatos* is each an apologia, though the interest of the first is rather for the student of our drama than the general reader, and we have had some hesitation in including it; but for such a reader the interest is very real. Jonson wrote quite deliberately for what we often call to-day a "highbrow" audience; and in the judgement of such readers, or those who wished to be accounted so, he stood higher in esteem than Shakespeare; if not with popular audiences, the theatre which *Catiline* or *Volpone* emptied was crowded if Falstaff were on the bill. In approaching an academic audience Jonson felt himself in a position to speak out and defend the drama, as at least it ought to be. But there was a dual strain of criticism to be encountered, and he obviously met with both even at the Universities,—the artistic and the moral or religious, the criticism of the classically educated and of the puritanly minded. Jonson emerges in his favourite rôle as the defender of the drama as it ought in theory to be: "able to inform young men to all good disciplines, inflame grown men to all great virtues," etc. etc., but

7

also as a severe critic of the drama of his day, a condemnation from which even Shakespeare is not in all Ben's moods to be exempted, if in other fluctuations of his wayward temper he will commend him not alone for his genius but his art. Donne's *apologia* is of a more personal kind, and perhaps promises more than he has in the end the courage to carry through. It is from the bent of his own mind in moments when he, like others, looks round for an escape, that he is tempted to consider the possible legitimacy, in certain circumstances, of an act which, at least since St. Augustine, the Church has consistently condemned:—since we may apparently do many things by way of austere self-discipline which may or must shorten life, is it not possible that in certain circumstances it may not only be justifiable, but become a duty, to end one's life voluntarily? It was of his own will that Christ laid down his life on the Cross. St. Augustine had pronounced dogmatically that only if directly inspired by God might we—as Samson in destroying God's enemies, or women in defence of their honour—take the final act into our own hands; but Donne rejects the Saint's authority on this point. It "hath no ground in history." The Introduction or Preface is, frankly speaking, more interesting than the fine-spun piece of casuistry which constitutes the gist of the book. Essentially it is an appeal for charity in judging; and setting aside cases of social disgrace it is doubtful if suicide is ever committed in a state of mind entirely sane.

Apologies of another kind, and raising another question, are the prefaces we have culled from three young poets—the peasant, the nobleman, and the "cockney," each making his first bow to the public. Burns's is the most pathetic as his position is the most difficult, the peasant poet venturing beyond his "little clan" to appeal to more polite and learned readers. But the young nobleman is just as apologetic, if he is conscious of his rank as to some extent a line of retreat. The reception which Byron's first venture did receive awakened him to a more effective response as the satirist emerged, who is all himself in the later, by some twenty years, dedication to *Don Juan*. The most simple and sincere is that of Keats. "The nameless worm," cries Shelley in *Adonais*, that is the critic in *Blackwood*:

would now itself disown:
It felt, yet could escape, the magic tone
Whose prelude held all envy, hate, and wrong
But what was howling in one breast alone,
Silent with expectation of the song,
Whose master's hand is cold, whose silver lyre unstrung.

The question raised by these deprecatory addresses is this:—I have said above, citing Keble and Mill, that while the orator's aim is to excite and direct the feelings of his audience, the poet's is to express, to communicate his own, to awaken response. Both poets and critics have spoken at times as if the poet were indifferent to an audience, were content in speaking to himself. Well, these prefaces speak for themselves. As Nietzsche says, "Lonely thinking, that is wise; lonely singing stupid." What distinguishes the poet from the orator, the rhetorician, is the *kind* of audience he desires, the *kind* of response. Here he draws closer to the man of science. A Galileo, a Darwin, an Einstein may, or may not, be elated or depressed by the reaction to his work of the general public. What he wants is the response of his fellow scientists, their acceptance and approval. He may not always get it at once; but there is to-day a large body of opinion able to assess and appreciate sooner or later. The poet in like manner desires an intelligent response, an echo in the hearts and imaginations of those who have ears to hear. In that quest he is more at the mercy of changing fashions than is the scientist. The poet's best judges are, or ought to be, his fellow poets, but this is not always the case at once, witness Shelley's failure quite to appreciate Keats and the like failure of Keats quite to comprehend Shelley. The failure to find an echo in the hearts and imaginations of his fellow men is the burthen of Shelley's most musical laments, if in his mind it is the prophet as well as the poet who would fain be heard:

Away! away! from man and towns
To the wild wood and the downs—
To the silent wilderness
Where the soul need not repress
Its music, lest it should not find
An echo in another's mind,

9

> *While the touch of Nature's art*
> *Harmonises heart to heart.*

That is the cry of the poet. The prophet desires something more:

> *Drive my dead thoughts over the universe*
> *Like withered leaves, to quicken a new birth!*
> *And, by the incantation of this verse,*
> *Scatter, as from an unextinguished hearth*
> *Ashes and sparks, my words among mankind!*

Shelley, in 1820, had little hope of any response in English periodicals, and the Preface to the *Prometheus* is mainly elucidatory. It falls into three parts which I have separated in printing as the significance of the third section has not been fully appreciated till recently. In the first he explains his treatment of the myth, wherein and why he has diverged from the reported treatment of the same by Aeschylus in his lost tragedy. In the second the main theme is his own style or imagery in relation to the poetry of the Greeks on the one hand and of his contemporaries on the other. Of the latter the greatest and most important in Shelley's eyes were Wordsworth and Byron. In his Preface to *The Cenci* a year later Shelley states clearly his attitude towards the theory of style expounded by Wordsworth: "I have written more carelessly; that is without an over-fastidious choice of words. In this respect I entirely agree with those modern critics who assert that in order to move men to true sympathy we must use the familiar language of men, and that our great ancestors the ancient English poets are the writers, a study of whom might incite us to do that for our age which they have done for theirs. But it must be the real language of men in general and not that of any particular class to whose society the writer happens to belong." It is the third section beginning "Let this opportunity," etc., whose significance has not till quite recently been fully realised. The *Prometheus* was *not* composed, like the drama of Aeschylus, as a philosophic and religious drama without immediate relevance. It was written with an immediate purpose, to prepare the minds of the young and generous to give to the revolution, which Shelley believed to be approaching, the guidance of the spirit of love and forbearance, that it may not lose itself in a chaos of violence and cruelty, leading back to tyranny, as the French Revolution had done.

Shelley is not the only poet who has thought of himself as a prophet; we have touched already on Milton. Indeed it might be disputed if Shelley should not rather be called, in Mr. Toynbee's phrase, a "futurist," the opposite of the "antiquarian," one who does not look back for the Golden Age but forward to a good time to come of necessity, some how, and some when. For the true *differentia* of the prophet is not that he can read the future, like some Zadkiel's Almanac, but that he has, and gives us, a deeper insight into the constitution of man in his relation to God, on the right understanding and acceptance of which must depend the ultimate fate of the race, not propitiatory sacrifices, human or animal, but "to do justly, and to love mercy, and to walk humbly with thy God," which the Christian would interpret as including to accept humbly what He has done for you. If Shelley is a prophet in this sense it will be in the stress he lays upon love. But Wordsworth comes nearer to Milton in his blend of the two, and it is to emphasise this that we have made our selections, leaving out as much as we could of the more purely literary theory, such as his thoughts on metre. The two strains are perhaps even more subtly blended in Wordsworth than in Milton, for it is both on poetical and prophetic grounds that he bases his plea for a simpler diction. It brings the language of poetry closer to the manner in which we do, or would if we could, express ourselves under the direct influence of a moving experience; and it is better adapted to Wordsworth's aim as prophet or teacher, the democratic purpose in his choice of subject which he states singly and precisely in the letter to Fox. To use the actual language of men in preference to a pompous phraseology confined to metrical composition is the same thing as to wear one's own hair instead of a powdered wig; and Wordsworth himself had been one of the Cambridge students who astonished Dorothy by their "smart powdered heads with black caps like helmets, only that they have a square piece of wood at the top, and gowns something like those that clergymen wear" (*Dorothy Wordsworth*, by E. de Selincourt, p. 22).

Blake too was a poet and in his own judgement a prophet of the apocalyptic kind represented by the Book of Daniel in the *Old Testament*. We have not ventured into the obscurities of the Prophetic Epics, but we have included the Preface to *Milton* which, with *Jerusalem*, has been the favourite quarry of Blake's expositors. It marks clearly the reversion to Christianity which followed his stay at Felpham: "Though I have been very unhappy, I am so no longer. I have again emerged into the light of day. I still and shall to Eternity embrace Christianity, and adore Him who is the express image of God . . ." Accordingly in this brief and characteristically passionate preface, like Milton when he came to write *Paradise Regained*, Blake rejects all the wisdom of Greece and Rome. Blake had never been the classical scholar that Milton was, but Blake could not express his rejection more precisely than Milton does in the words of Christ:

> *Alas! what can they teach, and not mislead;*
> *Ignorant of themselves, of God much more,*
> *And how the world began, and how man fell*
> *Degraded by himself, on grace depending.*

Neither of them knew or realised how much Christian tradition and thought owed to Greek philosophy, to Plato even before, with St. Thomas, Aristotle became the Christian Apologist and philosopher. One may doubt if Milton would quite have accepted Blake's reading of Christianity. In part, one feels, heretic was drawn to heretic.

Sir Walter Scott was the last of authors to claim prophetic inspiration or burden. In reading Lockhart's *Life* one is tempted to wish that Scott and Wordsworth could have been a little compounded, blended (they had as a fact some common sympathies), a little of Scott's detachment lent to Wordsworth, of Wordsworth's serious interest in his art to Scott. There was a vein of deeper feeling in Scott than is always apparent on the bright and shining surface, a vein that made Ruskin declare that "of all poetry I know, none is so sorrowful as Scott's." But the general tone of his introductions is simply informative, sensible, and touched with humour, a humour that in some of the later introductions (in which he poses as this or that worthy) has a little too much of facetiousness. We have ventured to give one brief glimpse of the sadder vein from the epilogue to *The Lady of the Lake* and to select from the too long Introductory Letter to *The Fortunes of Nigel* those paragraphs in which he replies to the three charges being brought against him by his publishers (and the Captain of the dialogue is Constable), by the Booksellers and by the Critics,—first that he is pouring out the novels too closely on each other's heels; secondly, that the novels themselves are too hastily composed, want a well-constructed plot converging to an end; and thirdly, that he is writing for money. It was either Beethoven or Goethe who threw down one of the later novels and exclaimed "the man is writing for money," and Coleridge, who was more willing to live on other people's money, reiterated the charge in the hour of the tragic failure. Scott's answer to each charge is frank and sensible. But it does not touch what was the real trouble. It was not the *making* of money which involved Scott and his publishers in trouble. It was the *anticipation* of money, the spending in advance of money not yet earned. But the chief interest of the extracts is the description of the novelist's way of working, which is that, one suspects, of many creative minds.

To descend from the elevation of poets and prophets, the interest of several of these prefaces is the vivid reflection they render of the author's character. Perhaps none are more delightful than those of More and Johnson, because both are so pervaded by humanity and humour. As men indeed, they represented some of the finest and most amiable traits of specifically English character, if in the great Doctor these were not infrequently obscured by some deficiency of manners. Swift admired More, and it is quite in Swift's manner that More gives the impression at once of veracity and invention by his anxiety about details, and not least by the order of his inquiries. "I have forgotten to ascertain the exact breadth of a river, and, by the way, also to ask where in the New World Utopia is to be found." And when More came to his probable readers, are we to take him as entirely serious or, again like Swift, as a little parodying the manner in which writers are inclined to complain of their readers past or to come? What Swift would not or could not have done was to interweave with all this mystification a lovely picture of his own home life.   All is conveyed with the same air of candour.

Johnson, closing his long and exacting piece of work, cannot but look back on all it has meant to himself in expectation, in execution, and now in retrospect,—how he awoke from the dreams of a poet to find himself a lexicographer.   He is well aware of what he has to expect of readers who may use his work; and then he recalls with a sigh those to whom his work would have been a personal source of pride and congratulation.   I do not know that Johnson ever wrote anything that was more evenly balanced and sustained throughout than this preface.   It is so solidly based on the knowledge he has widened and deepened in the course of his work; his mind apprehends so clearly and he states so precisely the various considerations involved; the whole is pervaded with so dignified a strain of feeling, serious, humorous, pathetic.   "I never read this preface," said Horne Tooke, "but it makes me shed tears."   None of his stronger prejudices, the bats which, as Mr. Pearsall Smith puts it, haunted the great belfry of his brain, are dominant, nor any of his elaborate hyperboles, for to Johnson an hyperbole was a work of art which, like Homer's similes, made him forget his subject in the enjoyment of his powers as an artist.[1]

The most human in its self-revealing character is Boswell's Preface to his *Account of Corsica* (1765), especially that prefixed to the third edition if we take with it the closing paragraph of the earlier, in which he confessed what were his ambitions as an author. Did ever anyone give himself away quite so simply and completely? To acquire fame as an author will assure one a reputation which need not be sustained by too rigidly good behaviour, will make one respected without always having to be respectable.   This is the

---

[1] Every reader of Johnson knows how the death of Garrick "eclipsed the gaiety of nations," and how, to acquire a good style, one "must give his days and nights to the study of Addison."   But the gem is that on his friend the Bohemian poet, Savage: "On a bulk, in a cellar, or in a glasshouse among thieves and beggars, was to be found the author of *The Wanderer*, the man of exalted sentiments, extensive views, and curious observations: the man whose remarks on life might have assisted the statesman, whose ideas of virtue might have enlightened the moralist, whose eloquence might have influenced senates, and whose delicacy might have polished courts."

same Boswell as describes himself in the *Journal of a Tour in the Highlands* as "having all Dr. Johnson's principles with some degree of relaxation." But anyone who knows his *Boswell* at all well will see, looking back to this preface, all his characteristics: family pride, piety of a kind, knowledge of his own besetting weaknesses, ambition to be an author and to know great men, melancholia. Indeed, in the light of his later achievement one can detect in this preface the qualities which went to make Boswell a unique biographer, unique for his *Life of Johnson* is still the only biography which combines with truth the interest of a good novel, the life not told you about or analysed or judged but shown you just as Boswell saw it himself in varying scenes and situations. In commenting on the character of Paoli as Boswell has described it in the *Corsica*, Gray writes in a letter to Walpole: "Of Mr Boswell's truth I have not the least suspicion because I am sure he could invent nothing of the kind. The true title of this part of the work is a Dialogue between a Green Goose and a Hero." That is one side. Boswell was quite incapable of inventing a character such as Paoli or Johnson. He could from long familiarity work up the notes he had taken so as to give a vivid representation of Johnson's habitual manner of speaking. When he tries to talk in the same manner himself he is not infrequently fatuous. But also he could not conceal. Just as he is quite candid about himself, his vanities and weaknesses, so he will record all he knows about Johnson be it to Johnson's or his own credit or not, with no parade, but as a disinterested artist who will let nothing revealing escape him. Lockhart would have thought it beneath his dignity to be so self-defacing or self-debasing as Boswell could be for the sake of his hero and his work. On the other hand Lockhart will invent scenes, in which he himself plays a part, that have no basis in fact.

In some of our prefaces one gets both the personal note and an interest that goes beyond, involves other and wider interests. Trollope's preface comes at the end of his series of clerical tales, but that, as we have seen, does not alter its character as a preface. It has an interest not only from the light it throws on Trollope's character, though one may doubt if he is so indifferent to the religious side of his characters as he professes. It is not difficult in this series and in other novels, for example *Miss Mackenzie*, to detect his dislike of Evangelical emotionalism and of long sermons. But the preface has an interest also for the larger question of the treatment in literature, and indeed for the study of the lives, of those who, in Goldsmith's words, combine the "three greatest characters upon earth—priest, father of a family, and husbandman," a combination which quite certainly creates problems not too easy of solution for the individual, be he Archdeacon Grantley or another. The Church of Rome, basing its teaching on the seventh chapter of the first Epistle to the Corinthians, where Paul affirms "I would that ye were all even as myself" but concedes that "it is better to marry than to burn," decreed in course of time for its clergy the duty of celibacy, and produced thereby another type of clerical character, the study of which in literature can be interesting.

The verses with which Morris introduces his *Earthly Paradise* have also a wider than the immediate personal interest. Morris was not content to remain the idle singer of an empty day. It is a short-sighted criticism which regards the so-called Pre-Raphaelite movement as a merely artistic escape, the shutting-up of the poet in an ivory tower of art for art. It was more than that, as the life of Morris was to show. It was a protest against the ugliness, physical and moral, of the world of industrialism, and against the utilitarian morality of the dominant middle classes, against also, consciously or unconsciously, the increasing secularisation of life, the gradual extinction of the blend of great truths and great dreams which had given beauty and sublimity to the life and poetry of the Middle Ages despite the great and manifest evils of the same ages. All of the group, the Rossettis, Dante and Christina, William Morris, even Swinburne and, outside the actual group, Ruskin, Patmore, High Churchmen and Ritualists—they were all in their different ways seekers after a City, escapists from a noisy but empty world (which has fallen in ruins about us), escapists if you like, but at times escape, flight, is the only form the prophet's protest can take. "It is enough now O Lord, take away my life: for I am not better than my fathers."

Matthew Arnold was, if not a prophet, a teacher with a message for the England of the century, but he chose as his masters and models Socrates and Plato rather than Jeremiah. We have selected a short preface, and further shortened it because the immediate occasion, the Land Bill of 1881 which established the principle of dual ownership in land, is now very ancient history. Short as it is, the preface states succinctly and sufficiently what had been the specific message of Arnold in all that he had to say to the English people in his many social and religious essays or treatises, *Culture and Anarchy, Friendship's Garland, Ecce Convertimur ad Gentiles, The Future of Liberalism*, etc. (I leave aside the religious studies). We have had enough, even too much, was Arnold's cry, of the Hebraic, prophetic, denunciatory criticism of Carlyle, Ruskin, and others. What we English need is rather more of the Hellenic spirit, of lucidity of mind and largeness of temper. "Think! think! and in conduct, political or private, cultivate more of the beautiful, the amiable." "Cultivate equality and shun greed" in private and in national dealings alike. What Arnold says about the Irish resentment of the treatment dealt out to them by English visitors for the pleasure of hunting, and the Irish short-sightedness, to English eyes, in not sufficiently appreciating the money which it brought with it, is recognisable by other than the Irish. On a yachting cruise with Oxford friends many years ago one of us recalls turning over the pages of a book on sport in the Western Highlands, and reading the advice to the sportsmen to have nothing to do with the natives, "a surly and disagreeable race." Such was too often the attitude of that public-school Englishman, the sportsman.

But it is difficult to indicate all the different features that may give piquancy to the personal note in a preface. It may be a strong vein of prejudice in the delightfully conservative Peacock. The conservative mind, by which is not meant the mind of a Conservative politician but an inborn instinct of resistance to change just as such, is an interesting phenomenon. Croker and Lockhart were gravely concerned over the revolutionary effects of a penny postage. A letter of the late Professor Saintsbury left one puzzled as to whether the loss of our forces at Kut or the introduction of Summer Time was the more to be deplored. But Peacock's conservative instincts by no means disturb his gaiety, or narrow his sympathies with so ardent a champion of reform as

17   c

Shelley. It was to him that many of the best of Shelley's letters from Italy were addressed; and to him we owe the *Defence of Poetry*. But if there is such a thing as a conservative bent or twist of mind, there is a liberal, a reforming *ditto*, and it too is not always to be sought in the political Liberal. "I have a passion for reforming the world," writes Shelley. There was a measure of the same passion in the Reverend Sydney Smith, if less idealistic, more practical and English. Over against Peacock's humorous arraignment of reformers as "fools" (to use the epithet favoured by Peacock's editor, the late Professor Saintsbury) we may set the genial figure of the first editor of *The Edinburgh Review*. His high-spirited survey of the long battle he had waged with privilege, injustice, and cruelty ends delightfully in the discovery that Whigs and Liberals in power find support from quite unexpected sources. "I never knew I had so many friends," did not someone say on coming unexpectedly into property? Or to put it from the other side: "The rich and powerful live in a perpetual masquerade, in which all about them wear borrowed characters; and we only discover in what estimation we are held, when we can no longer give hopes or fears" (*Johnson*). That is what the poor Liberal Party is discovering to-day, while the Labour Party must survey with satisfaction, blended with a little amusement, the stream of recruits.

George Eliot's meditation on the St. Teresas in the lives and histories of women gains a new interest from our growing knowledge of her own life and character. She too was a St. Teresa in her ideals, but like her own Mrs. Casaubon she was also a woman with all a woman's need for male companionship and support. It has often been charged against *Middlemarch*, her greatest novel, that it was a sad decline for her heroine to marry Ladislaw; but just so did George Eliot decline on a Chapman and a Lewis.

Of Ruskin, that rare and beautiful spirit, the reputation, whether as critic of art or the vindicator of the teaching of the Hebrew Prophets and the Gospel against an inhumanly abstract Political Economy, the identification of wealth and power with greatness, seems to be emerging from its dark night of oblivion and ridicule. The personal note, the note of feeling, pervades Ruskin's work as persistently as it does that of Milton, though Ruskin's is a less haughty, and fundamentally a sweeter, personality. We have taken our examples from a preface and some epilogues composed at critical epochs in the long history of his mental and spiritual growth. The first is the Preface to the original edition in 1842 of *Modern Painters*. If not exciting, it is of first-rate importance, indicating the impulse from which the work took its rise, and the larger character of the end he had in view than has always been appreciated. It is not a vindication of Turner alone, but is a claim for the greater truth to, and understanding of, Nature in the landscape art of the moderns when compared with that even of the famous artists of the past, and so a vindication of the honour of "those great living Masters whom we now neglect or malign, to pour our flattery into the ear of Death, and exalt, with vain acclamations, the names of those who neither demand our praise nor regard our gratitude." Our second is from the long Epilogue of 1883, forty years later, in which he recalls and recounts the journey that led him to his first contact with, and realisation of, the full greatness of the art of Venice, the "Venetian school which," Reynolds had declared, "may be said to be the Dutch part of the Italian genius." Ruskin had not been an admirer of the Dutch artists, not even Rembrandt. Our third is from the final Epilogue of 1888, in which, reviewing all he had done and suffered, all the vicissitudes of his Faith in God and in Art, he feels able to declare his unshaken loyalty to both: "Life without Industry is sin; and Industry without Art, brutality."

The prefaces which remain, and indeed the whole selection, may appear a somewhat miscellaneous lot unless it be remembered what exactly has been our guiding star. It is neither the interest of subject-matter in itself nor style for its own sake, but always personal feeling and character. Thus Dryden has been somewhat of a problem. In no writer perhaps have the personal interest and that of subject-matter been so closely blended. Dryden had interests other than literature, even religion and politics, both in the main determined by the personal needs of the moment. He was ever ready to trim his sails to the changes of wind and writes on each tack with apparent conviction. As Scott says, "Dryden knew how to assume every style which fitted the occasion." But literature was his Delilah, from the Heroic Drama at the outset to translation at the end. On each fashion of the moment he loved to elaborate critical theories interesting if, with other things, not to be adhered to with a fatiguing consistency. These have been collected and commented on by the late W. P. Ker. Dryden is almost the father of English criticism, except it be Ben Jonson. But a change came over the tone of his dedications when after the Revolution he, like Milton after the Restoration, fell on evil days:

On evil days though fall'n and evil tongues.

Then the personal note becomes more personal, first in the fine but long dedication of *Don Sebastian* (1690) to the Earl of Leicester, whom he praises as one who "in every turn of state, without meddling on either side, has always been favourable and assisting to oppressed merit"; then in that of *Amphitryon* to Sir William Leveson Gower where, growing a little sulky, he declares his resolve to address "only such as have been pleased to own me in this ruin of my small fortune." For *King Arthur* (1691) he chose the great Trimmer, the Marquis of Halifax, whose defeat of the Exclusion Bill had, he maintained, saved the country from civil war: "So many wives who have yet their husbands in their arms; so many parents who have not the number of their children lessened; so many villages, towns, and cities, whose inhabitants are not decreased, their property violated, or their wealth diminished, are yet owing to the sober conduct and happy results of your advice." In that which we have chosen Dryden's spirits are recovering, a hope awakening that he may find a patron even at Court, for the Earl of Rochester addressed is not the wicked Earl to whom *Marriage à la mode* was dedicated in 1673, who later had Dryden beaten on the street, but the son of the Earl of Clarendon and the uncle of Queen Mary. Dryden's outrageous, but always eloquent, flattery is here pervaded by a strain of elegance in touching on the ladies of the family and on poetry which more than compensates.

From the later Tennyson we have taken two dedicatory poems. The early Tennyson was the artist pure and simple, his subjects fanciful, even trifling. The maturer poet of the middle years was too consciously anxious to be the prophet and teacher of his age.

But in the last poems he voices the disillusionment of the author of first *Locksley Hall* in tones at times hysterical but also in deeply moving poems, and on no subject does he write with more feeling than the thought of death, which, as with Swift and Johnson and many others, was seldom out of his mind: "The reflections upon it begin when I wake in the morning and end when I go to sleep" (*Swift*). "The whole of life is but keeping away the thought of death" (*Johnson*). The tone of many of these poems does not differ greatly from that of Horace:

> *But thou art silent under ground,*
> *And o'er thee streams the rain.*
>
> *Omnes eodem cogimur*, etc.
>
>   *All must tread*
> *One common path, the highway of the dead:*
> *Fate shakes the urn, and o'er the Stygian river*
> *Soul after Soul to exile fleets forever.*
>   (*Sir Stephen de Vere*)

Tennyson clung intellectually to the hope of immortality, a modified Christian faith. But science, it seemed to Tennyson, was confirming Horace's conviction after centuries of Christian hopes and fears:

What be these two shapes high over the sacred fountain,
Taller than all the Muses, and huger than all the mountain?

.   .   .   .   .

Look, in their deep double shadow the crowned ones all disappearing.
Sing like a bird and be happy! nor hope for a deathless hearing
"Sounding for ever and ever"; pass on, the sight confuses.
These are Astronomy and Geology, terrible Muses.

Doughty, as his name promised, was a more fearless *Nasrany*, refusing the smallest concession to the fanaticism that would have deemed it a sacred duty to murder the heretic: "Ha, son of mischief, how long dost thou refuse the religion of Islam. . . . Except thou say this testimony thou wilt be slain to-day; thou gettest no more grace, for many have determined to kill thee." Yet Doughty found, among the wild Bedouin, Humanity that could hold its own against Faith: "Righteousness, justice, sanctity, spring naturally in the human conscience; they are lent to the religions, wherein divinity and human equity stand oft-times so far asunder that we might muse of a stone age in their supposed heaven."

Mary Kingsley found a little of the same among the cannibal Fan tribes of West Africa, though not to be too much "lippened to": "I never found him [the Fan] treacherous; but then I never trusted him, remembering one of the aphorisms of my great teacher Captain Boler of Bonny, 'It's not safe to go among bush tribes, but if you are such a fool as to go, you needn't go and be a bigger fool still, you've done enough.'" Even a short preface by that great and delightful woman and author is enough to show character and humour sufficient for any collector. It may be that in her volume, as she hints, a pedantic stickler for rules of agreement and government, and the distinction between "shall" and "will," may be worried. A less fastidious grammarian will find more than sufficient to compensate in happy description and image, and, in the sentence, what is of more importance in English than agreement and government, a natural order of words and a right distribution of emphasis. But I am tempted to add to this brief prelude one fragment from her book which is eloquent of her courage, humour, and insight: "My favourite form of literature . . . is accounts of mountaineering exploits, though I have never seen a glacier or a permanent snow mountain in my life. I do not care a row of pins how badly they may be written, and what form of bumble-puppy grammar and composition is employed, as long as the writer will walk along the edge of a precipice; or better still with a sheer fall of thousands of feet on the one side and a precipice on the other; or better still crawl up an arête with a precipice on either. Nothing on earth would persuade me to do either of these things myself, but they remind me of bits of country I have been through where you walk along a narrow line of security with gulfs of murder looming on each side, and where, in exactly the same way, you are as safe as if you were in your easy-chair at home, as long as you get sufficient holding ground: not on rock in the bush village inhabited by murderous cannibals, but on ideas in those men's and women's minds; and these ideas I think I may say you will always find give you safety. It is not advisable to play with them, or to attempt to eradicate them, because you regard them as superstitious; and never, never shoot too soon. I have never had to shoot and hope never to have to; because in such a situation, one white alone with no troops to back him means a clean finish. But this would not discourage me, if I had to start, only it makes me more inclined to walk round the obstacle than to become a mere blood splotch against it, if this can be done without losing your self-respect, which is the mainspring of your power in West Africa." Thackeray in the Preface to *Pendennis* describes a not dissimilar feat of balancing on the narrow edge of Victorian proprieties which the novelist of his day had to tread. He was forbidden the larger and more truthful picture of life enjoyed by his eighteenth-century predecessors. We have broken away from all that now, not always in the most engaging way, for we do not leaven the whole with a strain of humour.

Some of the remaining prefaces may be left to speak for themselves—Hale White's re-echo of the wisdom of *Ecclesiastes*; Robert Louis Stevenson's championship of youth. We have chosen Yeats's account of his transition from lyrical poetry to drama, if indeed he did succeed in effecting the transition. It has at any rate a wider interest than his more personal compliments to his ancestors or disquisitions on Gyrations, though indeed he can make poetry of both. And finally, of men of letters, Thomas Hardy. His preface to *Late Lyrics and Earlier* is the fullest and most touching expression of his attitude to the problems of life with which he had wrestled in his novels at once sombre and humorous. It is in the light of what he says here that one might with profit re-read them all. For Hardy's confession of his attitude towards the loss of faith is the most sincere and human of all such outcries. He has added to it elsewhere by recalling his religious inheritance: "In this connection he said once . . . that although invidious critics had cast slurs upon him as Nonconformist, Agnostic, Infidel, Immoralist, Heretic, Pessimist or something else equally opprobrious in their eyes, they had never thought of calling him much more plausibly—'Churchy'; not in an intellectual sense, but in so far as instincts and emotions ruled. As a child to be a parson had been his dream, moreover he had several clerical relatives who held livings; while his grandfather, father, uncle, brother, wife, cousin, and two sisters had been musicians in various churches over a period covering altogether more than a hundred years. . . . He himself had frequently read the Church lessons, and had at one time as a young man begun reading for Cambridge with a view to taking orders." The fact is that losing his faith left Hardy somewhat in the plight of a hermit-crab which has outgrown its shell and must scuttle around in a very exposed condition till it can find a larger shell. That larger shell Hardy never found, but this preface suggests how sincerely he sought it.

Our intention had been not to transgress beyond poets and men of letters. But memory and interest suggested some search among philosophers. We have rested content with selections from Berkeley and Bradley. Berkeley's will seem a strange choice but it seemed to us interesting both historically and personally. The sermons brought against the preacher a charge of Jacobitism. But he was a loyal Hanoverian, though it nearly brought on him the fate of Thomas Sheridan in being deprived of advancement, as that unfortunate person was for inadvertently preaching on the anniversary of the arrival of William from the text, "Sufficient for the day is the evil thereof." Berkeley's interest was one of principle. To us its interest lies in the help it gives to a right appreciation of what the word "Tory" meant to a man of the eighteenth century such as Swift, Berkeley, Johnson, and one might add Dryden. A nickname to begin with, "Tory" came for these to mean an upholder of the established order in Church and State, a lover of order, a loyalist. The Whigs seemed to them essentially and historically republicans, potentially rebels. Satan was the first Whig. When after the French Revolution and under the influence of Burke many Whigs rallied to the other side, and when, in the age of Victoria, the middle classes became the dominant influence, the centre of gravity shifted somewhat from loyalty to the established order in Church and State to the sacred rights and privileges of property, and not surprisingly the name "Tory" gave way to "Conservative."

It is unnecessary to say anything of Bradley's great Preface, his claim for the study of metaphysics as at once a sceptical protection against superstition religious or materialist, but also as one, though not the only one, of the paths along which some minds trave. towards an apprehension of the Absolute. Professor Taylor, who speaks with the authority of friend and thinker, has said: "It may be said of him [Bradley] as was said by Byron of Shelley, a poet for whom he had a lifelong love, that he had framed an ideal and lived up to it 'to the letter'. . . . It is a saying of his own that for some men metaphysics is a way of experiencing the Divine. With him this was pre-eminently so. The purely intellectual value of his metaphysical construction must be left to time to determine; for himself the speculative life had the incommunicable personal value of all forms of the mystic way."

"So here for the present the story stays." We have doubtless omitted several prefaces, etc. which a wider reading, or better memory (and we grow old), or necessary permission might have given us. Our publisher has been very patient with our occasional additions. One difficulty (apart from such a physical inhibition as length) might just be mentioned. To seek the personal note in the preface or epilogue to such an autobiography as, say, Newman's great *Apologia* was vain, for it was impressed on, diffused throughout, the whole work. The same is true of such books as *The Anatomy of Melancholy, Tristram Shandy, A Sentimental Journey,* and *Sartor Resartus.* Some novelists have cultivated, or indulged, the habit (derived perhaps from the immortal work of Cervantes) of talking from time to time with the reader over the head of the story and the characters. With Thackeray it became, in his later novels, almost a vice, disturbing the effect which Scott declared to Maria Edgeworth should be the aim of the novelist, to give the impression that the story is a chapter from the history of actual happenings. Thackeray *will* speak of his characters as puppets which at the end are to be laid aside. His great predecessor, Fielding, confined such personal comments generally to the preludes with which he ushers in each Book in his picture of a young man's life, *Tom Jones.* All of them are full of character, and it seemed difficult to choose. But finally we have selected one in which there is a deeper note of feeling, which gives the impression I have referred to earlier of something that he was determined to say breaking through, the prelude on Love. Here he states and defends that element in his picture of life which Thackeray complains it is forbidden to the Victorian to touch on. But he does so as one who believes passionately in the power of genuine love to absorb and transcend the sensuous element, to omit reference to which is to falsify or shirk the facts of life. Looking back I find I have given no reason for our including Dryden's eulogy of Shakespeare, prefixed to his recast of Davenant's version of *The Tempest*, in an anthology entitled *The Personal Note*. What is personal in these lines? It is the unqualified estimate of Shakespeare as the greatest of our dramatists. An American critic[1] has recently proved, by a detailed examination, what any student of the seventeenth century must have noticed or suspected, that throughout the century Ben Jonson was, in critical judgement, accepted as our leading dramatist. There might be an occasional exception such as John Hales, just as there might be and were occasional critics of the Victorian century who preferred Browning or Arnold to Tennyson. But for Pepys at the Restoration Jonson is sacrosanct, Shakespeare may be criticised like any other. What interests him is not *Hamlet* but Betterton in *Hamlet*. In his own first challenge to this estimate, *The Essay on Dramatic Poesy* (1668), Dryden's language is slightly apologetic. Asked to analyse *The Silent Woman*, he refers to Shakespeare and Fletcher as Jonson's "rivals in poesy; and one of them, in my opinion, at least his equal, perhaps his superior." In these lines, a year later, there is no qualification:

> *But Shakespeare's magic could not copied be;*
> *Within that circle none durst walk but he.*

To hear that Shakespeare had taught him art was enough to make Jonson turn in his grave, he who had told Drummond that "Shakespeare wanted art."

The idea of such an anthology was suggested by my partner and friend of past days, and did seem to me to promise a kind of interest different from, if less exciting than, a similar anthology of Invective and Abuse.

H. J. C. GRIERSON

[1] *Shakespeare and Jonson, Their Reputations in the Seventeenth Century Compared.* Gerard Eaves Bentley. University of Chicago Press, 1945.

GEOFFREY CHAUCER

CANTERBURY TALES

I

Prelude to The Tale of Sir Thopas

HIS SELF-PORTRAIT

WHEN seyd was al this miracle, every man
As sobre was, that wonder was to se,
Til that our hoste Iapen tho bigan,
And than at erst he loked up-on me,
And seyde thus, What man artow? quod he;
Thou lokest as thou woldest finde an hare,
For ever up-on the ground I see thee stare.

Approche neer, and loke up merily,
Now war yow, sirs, and lat this man have place;
He in the waast is shape as wel as I;
This were a popet in an arm t'embrace
For any womman, smal and fair of face.
He semeth elvish by his countenance,
For unto no wight dooth he daliaunce.

Sey now somwhat, sin other folk han seyd;
Tel us a tale of mirthe, and that anoon;
"Hoste," quod I, "ne beth nat yvel apayd,
For other tale certes can I noon,
But of a ryme I lerned long agoon."
"Ye, that is good," quod he; "now shul we here
Som deyntee thing, me thinketh by his chere."

II

Epilogue to The Tale of the Parson

HERE TAKETH THE MAKERE OF THIS BOOK HIS LEVE

Now preye I to hem alle that herkneth this litel tretis or rede, that if ther be any thing in it that lyketh hem, that ther-of they thanken oure lord IESU CRIST, of whom procedeth al wit and al goodnesse. And if ther be any thing that displese hem I prey hem also that they arrete it to the defaute of myn unconninge, and nat to my wil, that wolde ful fayn have seyd bettre if I hadde had conninge. For oure boke seith al that is writen is writen for oure doctrine; and that is myn entente. Wherfore I biseke yow mekely for the mercy of God, that ye preye for me, that Crist have mercy on me and foryeve me my giltes: and namely of my translacions and endytinges of worldly vanities, the whiche I revoke in my retracciouns: as is the book of Troilus; The book also of Fame; The book of the nyneteen Ladies; The Book of the Duchesse; The book of seint Valentynes day of the Parlement of Briddes; The tales of Canterbury, thilke that sounen in-to sinne; The Book of the Leoun; and many another book, if they were in my remembrance, and many a song and many a lecherous lay; that Crist for his grete mercy foryeve me the sinne. But of the translacion of Boece de Consolacione, and other bokes of legendes of seintes, and omelies, and moralitee, and devocioun, that thanke I oure lord Iesu Crist and his blisful Moder, and alle the seintes of hevene; biseking hem that they from hennes-forth, unto my lyves ende, sende me grace to biwayle my giltes and to studie to the salvacioun of my soule:— and graunte me grace of verray penitence, confessioun and satisfaccioun to doon in this present lyf; thurgh the benigne grace of him that is king of kinges and preest over alle preestes, that boghte us with the precious blood of his herte; so that I may been oon of hem at the day of dome that shulle be saved: *Qui cum patre &c.*

SIR THOMAS MORE
UTOPIA
Englished by Ralph Robynson
1551

Thomas More to Peter Giles sendeth gretynge

I AM almoste ashamed, righte wellbeloved Peter Giles, to send unto you this boke of the Utopian commonwealth, welnigh after a yeres space, whiche I am sure you looked for within a moneth and a halfe. And no marveil. For you knew well ynough, that I was already disburdened of all the laboure and studye belonging to the invention in this worke, and that I had no nede at al to trouble my braines about the disposition or conveiance of the matter: and therfore had herein nothing else to do but only to rehearse those thinges which you and I together hard maister Raphael tell and declare. Wherefore there was no cause why I should study to set forth the matter with eloquence: forasmuch as his talke could not be fine and eloquent, beynge firste not studied for, but sudden and unpremeditate, and then, as you know, of a man better seen in the Greek language than in the Latin tongue. And my writynge, the nigher it should approach to his homely plaine and simple speche, so much the nigher should it go to the truth : which is the only mark whereunto I do and ought to directe all my travail and study herin.

I graunte and confesse, frende Peter, myself discharged of so much laboure havinge all these thinges ready done to my hande, that almoost there was nothinge left for me to do. Elles either the invention or the disposition of this matter mighte have required of a wit neither base, neither at all unlearned, both some time and leasure, and also some studie. But if it were requisite and necessarie, that the matter should also have bene wrytten eloquentlie, and not alone truely; of a suretie that thynge coulde I have perfourmed by no time nor studye. But now seinge all these cares, stayes, and lettes were taken awaye, wherein else so much laboure and studye shoulde have bene employed, and that there remayned no other thynge for me to do, but onelye to write playnely the matter as I hard it spoken: that indeed was a thynge lighte and easy to be done. Howbeit to the dispatchynge of this so little busynesse my other cares and troubles did leave almost lesse then no leasure. Whiles I do daylie bestowe my time about law matters: some to pleade, some to heare, some as an arbitratoure with mine award to determine, some as an umpier or a Judge with my sentence finally to discusse. Whiles I go one waye to see and visite my frende: an other waye about mine own privat affaires. Whiles I spende almost al the day abrode emonges others, and the residue at home among mine owne; I leave to my self, I meane to my booke, no time. For when I am come home I must commune with my wife, chatte with my children, and talk with my servauntes. All the which thinges I reckon and accompte amonge businesse, forasmuche as they must of necessitie be done: and done must they nedes be onlesse a man will be a straunger in his owne house. And in any wise a man must so fashioun and order his conditions, and so appoint and dispose him self, that he be merrie, jocunde, and pleasaunt amonge them whom, either nature hath provided, or chaunce hath made, or he him self, hath chosen to be the companyons of his life: so that with to much gentle behavioure and familiaritie, he do not mar them, and by to much sufferance of his servauntes make them his maysters. Emonge these thynges now rehearsed, stealeth awaye the daye, the moneth, the yeare. When do I write then? And all this while have I spoken no worde of slepe, neither yet of meate, which amonge a great number doth waste no less tyme, then doth slepe wherein almoste halfe the lifetime of man crepeth awaye. I therefore do wynne and get onlye that time which I steale from slepe and meate. Which tyme because it is very little, and yet somewhat it is, therefore have I ones at the last, though it be long first, finished Utopia; and have sent it to you, frende Peter, to reade and peruse: to the intent that if anye thinge have escaped me, you might put me in remembraunce of it. For though in this behalfe I do not greatlye mistruste myselfe (which woulde God I were somewhat in wit and learninge, as I am not all of the worste and dullest memorye) yet have I not so great truste and confidence in it that I thinke nothinge coulde fall out of my minde.

For John Clement my boye, who as you know was there present with us, whom I suffer to be awaye from no talke wherein may be any profyte or goodness (for out of this yonge bladed and new shotte up corne, which hath already begun to spring up both in Latin and Greke learning I loke for plentifull increase at length of goodly rype grayne) he I say hath broughte me into a greate doubte. For wheras Hythlodaye (onless my memorye faile me) sayde that the bridge of Amaurote, which goeth over the river of Anyder is fyve hundreth paseis, that is to say, half a myle in lengthe: my John sayeth that two hundred of those paseis must be plucked away, for that the ryver conteyneth there not above three hundreth paseis in breadth, I pray you hartely call the matter to your remembraunce. For yf you agree with hym, I also will saye as you saye, and confess myself deceaved. But if you cannot remember the thing, then surelye I will wryte as I have done, and as myne owne remembraunce serveth me. For as I will take good hede, that there be in my booke nothing false, so if there be anythynge doubtefull, I will rather tell a lye then make a lie: because I had rather be good then wittie. Howbeit this matter maye easily be remedied if you wyll take the paynes to aske the question of Raphael himself by woorde of mouthe, if he be nowe with you, or elles by youre letters. Which you must nedes do for another doubte also that hath chaunced, through whose faulte I cannot tell: whether through mine, or yours, or Raphaels. For neyther we rememebred to enquire of him, nor he to tell us in what part of the newe world Utopia is situate. The whiche thinge I had rather have spent no smalle somme of money then that it should thus have escaped us: aswell for that I am ashamed to be ignorant in what sea that ylande standeth, whereof I write so long a treatise, as also because there be with us certain men, and especially one vertuous and godly man, and a professour of divinitie, who is exceeding desirous to go to Utopia: not for a vayne and curious desire to see newes, but to the intente he may further and increase oure religion, which is there alreadye luckily begonne. And that he maye the better accomplyshe and perfourme this hys good intente he is minded to procure that he himself may be made Bishoppe of Utopia being nothing scrupulous herein that he muste obteyne this Bishopricke with suit. For he counteth that a godly suete which procedeth not of the desire of honoure or lucre, but onlie of godly zeale. Wherefore I moste earnestly desire you, frende Peter, to talke with Hythlodaye, if you can, face to face, or els to wryte youre letters to hym, and so to woorke in thys matter, that in this my booke there may neyther anythinge be founde whyche is untrue, neyther anythynge be lacking which is true. And I thynke vereleye it shalbe well done that you shewe unto him the booke itself. For yf I have myssed or fayled in anye poynte, or if anye faulte have escaped me, no man can so wel correcte and amende it as he can: and yet that can he not do onless he peruse, and reade over my book written. Moreover by this meanes shall you perceave whether he be well wylling and content, that I should undertake to put this worke in wryting. For if he be mynded to publyshe, and put forth his owne laboures, and travayles himselfe, perchaunce he woulde be lothe, and so would I also, that in publishynge the Utopiane weale publyke, I shoulde prevente him, and take from him the flower and grace of the noveltie of this his historie.

Howbeit, to saye the verye truth, I am not yet fullye determined with myself whether I will put forth my book or no. For the natures of men be so divers, the phantasies of some so waywarde, their myndes so unkynde, their judgementes so corrupte, that they which leade a merrie and a jocunde lyfe, folowinge theyr owne sensuall pleasures and carnall lustes, maye seme to be in a much better state or case then they that vexe and unquiete themselves with cares and studie for the putting forthe and publishynge of some thynge that may be either profeit or pleasure to others: which others nevertheless will disdainfully, scornefully, and unkindly accepte the same. The moost part of all be unlearned. And a greate number hathe learning in contempte. The rude and barbarous alloweth nothing but that which is verie barbarous in dede. If it be one that hath a little smacke of learninge, he rejecteth as homely geare and common ware whatsoever is not stuffed full of olde motheaten termes, and that be worne out of use. Some there be that have pleasure onlye in olde rusty antiquities. And some onlie in their owne doynges. One is so sowre, so crabbed, and so unpleasant that he can awaye with no myrthe nor sporte. An other is so narrowe betwene the shoulders, that he can beare no jestes nor tauntes. Some sely poore soules be so afearde that at everye snappish woorde their nose shall be bitten off, that they stande in no lesse dreade of everye quicke and sharpe woorde, than he that is bitten of a madde dogge feareth water. Some be so mutable and waveringe that every houre thay be in a newe mynde, sayinge one thinge syttinge, and another thinge standing. Another sorte sitteth upon their ale benches, and there amonge their cuppes they geve judgement of the wittes of writers, and with great authoritie they condempne even as pleaseth them everye writer accordinge to his writinge, in most spitefull manner mockynge, lowtinge, and flowtinge them; beinge themselves in the meane season sauffe, and as sayeth the proverbe, oute of all daunger of gunne shot. For why, they be so smugge and smothe, that they have not so much as one hearre [hair] of an honest man, whereby one may take hold of them. Ther be moreover some so unkinde and ungentle, that though they take great pleasure and delectation in the worke, yet for all that, they can not finde in their hertes to love the Author therof, nor to afford him a good woorde: beinge much like uncourteous, unthankfull, and chourlish guestes. Whiche when they have with good and daintie meates well fylled their bellyes, departe home, gevinge no thankes to the feaste maker. Go your wayes now, and make a costly feaste at your owne charges for guestes so dayntie mouthed, so divers in taste, and besides that of so unkinde and unthankfull natures. But nevertheless (frende Peter) do, I pray you, with Hythloday as I willed you before. And as for this matter I shall be at my libertie afterwards to take newe advisement. Howbeit, seeinge I have taken great paynes and laboure in wryting the matter, if it may stande with his mynde and pleasure, I will as touching the edition or publishing of the booke followe the counsell and advise of my frendes, and specially yours. Thus fare you well right hertely beloved frende Peter, with your gentle wife: and love me as you have ever done, for I love you better than ever I did.

SIR PHILIP SIDNEY

THE ARCADIA

1590

To my Deare Ladie and Sister, the Countesse of Pembroke

HERE now have you (most deare, and most worthy to be most deare Lady) this idle worke of mine: which I feare (like the Spiders webbe) will be thought fitter to be swept away, then worn to any other purpose. For my part, in very trueth (as the cruell fathers among the Greekes, were woont to doo to the babes they would not foster) I could well find in my harte, to caste out in some desert of forgetfulness this child, which I am loathe to father. But you desired me to doo it, and your desire, to my hart is an absolute commandement. Now, it is done onelie for you, onely to you: if you keepe it to your selfe, or to such friendes, who will weigh errors in the ballaunce of good will, I hope, for the fathers sake, it will be pardoned, perchance made much of, though in itselfe it have deformities. For indeede, for severer eyes it is not, being but a trifle, and that triflinglie handled. Your deare selfe can best witness the maner, being done in loose sheetes of paper, most of it in your presence, the rest, by sheetes, sent unto you, as fast as they were done. In summe, a young head, not so well stayed as I would it were, (and shall be when God will) having many many fancies begotten in it, if it had not ben in some way delivered, would have growen a monster, and more sorie might I be that they came in, then that they gat out. But his chiefe safetie, shalbe the not walking abroad; and his chiefe protection the bearing the liverie of your name; which (if much much good will do not deceave me) is worthy to be a sanctuary for a great offender. This say I, because I knowe the vertue so; and this say I, because it may be ever so; or to say better, because it will be ever so. Read it then at your idle times, and the follyes your good judgement wil finde in it, blame not, but laugh at. And so, looking for no better stuffe, then, as in an

34

Haberdashers shoppe, glasses, or feathers, you will continue to love the writer, who doth exceedinglie love you; and most most hartelie praies you may long live, to be a principall ornament to the familie of the Sidneis.

your loving Brother

Philip Sidnei

FRANCIS BACON

To Lord Treasurer Burghley

1591

MY LORD,

With as much confidence as mine own honest and faithful devotion
unto your service, and your honourable correspondence unto me
and my poor estate can breed in a man, do I commend myself unto
your lordship. I wax now somewhat ancient; one and thirty years
is a great deal of sand in the hour-glass. My health, I thank God,
I find confirmed; and I do not fear that action shall impair it;
because I account my ordinary course of study and meditation to be
more painful than most parts of action are. I ever bare a mind, in
some middle place that I could discharge, to serve her Majesty; not
as a man born under Sol, that loveth honour; nor under Jupiter,
that loveth business, for the contemplative planet carrieth me away
wholly: but as a man born under an excellent sovereign, that
deserveth the dedication of all men's abilities. Besides I do not find
in myself so much self-love, but that the greater part of my thoughts
are to deserve well, if I were able, of my friends, and namely of your
lordship; who being the Atlas of this commonwealth, the honour
of my house, and the second founder of my poor estate, I am tied
by all duties, both of a good patriot, and of an unworthy kinsman,
and of an obliged servant, to employ whatsoever I am to do you
service. Again, the meanness of my estate doth somewhat move
me: for though I cannot accuse myself, that I am either prodigal
or slothful, yet my health is not to spend, nor my course to get.
Lastly, I confess that I have as vast contemplative ends, as I have
moderate civil ends: for I have taken all knowledge to be my province; and if I could purge it of two sorts of rovers, whereof the one
with frivolous disputations, confutations, and verbosities; the other
with blind experiments and auricular traditions and impostures,
hath committed so many spoils; I hope I should bring in industrious
observations, grounded conclusions, and profitable inventions and
discoveries; the best state of that province. This, whether it be
curiosity, or vain glory, or nature, or if one take it favourably,

philanthropia, is so fixed in my mind as it cannot be removed. And I do easily see that place of any reasonable countenance doth bring commandment of more wits than of a man's own; which is the thing I greatly affect. And for your lordship, perhaps you shall not find more strength and less encounter in any other. And if your lordship shall find now or at any time, that I do seek or affect any place, whereunto any that is nearer unto your lordship shall be concurrent, say then that I am a most dishonest man. And if your lordship will not carry me on, I will not do as Anaxagoras did, who reduced himself with contemplation unto voluntary poverty: but this I will do, I will sell the inheritance that I have, and purchase some lease of quick revenue, or some office of gain, that shall be executed by deputy, and so give over all care of service, and become some sorry bookmaker, or a true pioneer in that mine of truth, which, he said, lay so deep. This which I have writ unto your lordship, is rather thoughts than words, being set down without all art, disguising, or reservation: wherein I have done honour both to your lordship's wisdom, in judging that that will be best believed of your lordship which is truest; and to your lordship's good nature in retaining nothing from you. And even so, I wish your lordship all happiness, and to myself means and occasion to be added to my faithful desire to do you service.

From my lodging at Gray's Inn

BEN JONSON
VOLPONE

To the Most Noble & Most Equall Sisters

THE TWO FAMOUS UNIVERSITIES

For Their Love And Acceptance
Shewn To His Poeme In The Presentation

BEN JONSON

The Grateful Acknowledger

DEDICATES BOTH IT AND HIMSELF

NEVER (most equal sisters) had any man a wit so presently excellent as that it could raise itself; but there must come both matter, occasion, commenders, and favourers to it. If this be true, and that the fortune of all writers doth daily prove it, it behoves the carefull to provide well towards these accidents; and, having acquired them, to preserve that part of reputation most tenderly, wherein the benefit of a friend is also defended. Hence is it, that I now render myself grateful, and am studious to justify the bounty of your act: to which, though your mere authority were satisfying, yet, it being an age wherein poetry, and the professors of it hear so ill, on all sides, there will a reason be looked for in the subject. It is certain, nor can it with any forehead be opposed, that the too much license of poetasters, in this time, hath much deformed their mistress; that, every day, their manifold, and manifest ignorance, doth stick unnatural reproaches upon her: But for their petulancy, it were an act of the greatest injustice, either to let the learned suffer; or so divine a skill (which indeed should not be attempted with unclean hands) to fall under the least contempt. For, if men will impartially, and not asquint, look toward the offices and function of a poet, they will easily conclude to themselves the impossibility of any man's being the good poet, without first being a good man. He that is said to be able to inform young men to all good disciplines, inflame grown men to all great virtues, keep old men in their best and supreme state, or, as they decline to childhood, recover them to their first strength; that comes forth the interpreter and arbiter of nature, a teacher of things divine no less than human, a master in manners; and can alone, or with a few, effect the business of mankind: This, I take him, is no subject for pride and ignorance to exercise their railing rhetoric upon. But it will here be hastily answered, that the writers of these days are other things; that not only their manners, but their natures, are inverted, and nothing remaining with them of the dignity of poet, but the abused name, which every scribe usurps; that now, especially in dramatic, or, as they term it, stage-poetry, nothing but ribaldry, profanation, blasphemy, all license of offence to God and man is practised. I dare not deny a great part of this, and am sorry I dare not, because in some men's abortive features (and would they had never boasted the light) it is over-true; but that all are embarked in this bold adventure for Hell, is a most uncharitable thought, and uttered, a more malicious slander. For my particular, I can, and from a most clear conscience, affirm, that I have ever trembled to think toward the least profaneness; have loathed the use of such foul and unwashed bawdry as is now made the food of the scene: and, howsoever I cannot escape from some the imputation of sharpness, but they will say, I have taken a pride, or lust, to be bitter, and not my youngest infant but hath come into the world with all his teeth; I would ask of these supercilious politics, what nation, society, or general order or state, I have provoked? What public person? Whether I have not in all these preserved their dignity, as mine own person, safe? My works are read, allowed, (I speak of those that are entirely mine) look into them, what broad reproofs have I used? where have I been particular? where personal? except to a mimic, cheater, bawd, or buffoon, creatures for their insolencies worthy to be taxed? yet to which of these so pointingly, as he might not either ingenuously have confest, or wisely dissembled his disease? But it is not rumour can make men guilty, much less entitle me to other men's crimes. I know, that nothing can be so innocently writ or carried, but may be made obnoxious to construction; marry, whilst I bear mine innocence about me, I fear it not. Application is now grown a trade with many; and there are that profess to have a key for the deciphering of everything: but let wise and noble persons take heed how they be too credulous, or give leave to these invading interpreters to be overfamiliar with their fames, who cunningly and often utter their own virulent malice under other men's simplest meanings. As for those that will (by faults which charity hath raked up, or common honesty concealed) make themselves a name with the multitude, or, to draw their rude and beastly claps, care not whose living faces they intrench with their petulant styles, may they do it without a rival for me! I choose rather to live graved in obscurity than share with them in so preposterous a fame. Nor can I blame the wishes of those severe and wise patriots, who providing the hurts these licentious spirits may do in a state desire rather to see fools and devils and those antique relics of barbarism retrieved, with all other ridiculous and exploded follies, than behold the wounds of private men, of princes and nations: for, as Horace makes Trebatius speak among these,

Sibi quisque timet, quanquam est intactus, et odit.

And men may justly impute such rages, if continued, to the writer, as his sports. The increase of which lust in liberty, together with the present trade of the stage, in all their miscelline interludes, what learned or liberal soul doth not already abhor? where nothing but the filth of the time is uttered, and with such impropriety of phrase, such plenty of solecisms, such derth of sense, so bold prolepses, so racked metaphors, with brothelry able to violate the ear of a pagan, and blasphemy to turn the blood of a Christian to water. I cannot but be serious in a cause of this nature, wherein my fame, and the reputation of divers honest and learned are the question; when a name so full of authority, antiquity, and all great mark, is, through their insolence become the lowest scorn of the age; and those men subject to the petulancy of every vernaculous orator, that were wont to be the care of kings and happiest monarchs. This it is that hath not only rapt me to present indignation, but made me studious heretofore, and by all my actions, to stand off from them; which may most appear in this my latest work, which you, most learned Arbitresses have seen, judged, and to my crown, approved; wherein I have laboured for their instruction and amendment, to reduce not only the ancient forms, but manners of the scene, the easiness, the propriety, the innocence, and last, the doctrine, which is the principal end of poesie, to inform men in the best reason of living. And though my catastrophe may, in the strict rigour of comic law, meet with censure, as turning back to my promise, I desire the learned and charitable critic, to have so much faith in me, to think it was done of industry: for, with what ease I could have varied it nearer his scale (but that I fear to boast my own faculty) I could here insert. But my special aim being to put the snaffle in their mouths that cry out, We never punish vice in our interludes &c. I took the more liberty; though not without some lines of example, drawn even in the ancients themselves, the goings out of whose comedies are not always joyful, but oftimes the bawds, the servants, the rivals, yea, and the masters are mulcted; and fitly, it being the office of a comic poet to imitate justice, and instruct to life, as well as purity of language, or stir up gentle affections; to which I shall take the occasion elsewhere to speak.

For the present, most reverenced Sisters, as I have cared to be thankful for your affections past, and here made the understanding acquainted with some ground of your favours; let me not despair their continuance, to the maturing of some worthier fruit; wherein if my muses be true to me, I shall raise the despised head of poetry again, and stripping her out of those rotten and base rags wherewith the times have adulterated her form, restore her to her primitive habit, feature, and majesty, and render her worthy to be embraced and kissed of all the great and master spirits of our world. As for the vile and slothful, who never affected an act worthy of celebration, or are so inward with their own vicious natures, as they worthily fear her, and think it an high point of policy to keep her in contempt with their declamatory and windy invectives; she shall out of just rage incite her servants (who are *genus irritabile*) to spout ink in their faces, that shall eat farther than their marrow into their fames; and not Cinnamus the barber, with his art, shall be able to take out the brands; but they shall live, and be read, till the wretches die, as things worst deserving of themselves in chief, and then of all mankind.

From my House in the Black-Friars,
this 11*th day of February,* 1607.

EDMUND SPENSER

THE FAERIE QUEENE
Last Words
From The VIIIth Canto Vnperfite

I

When I bethinke me on that speech whyleare,
  Of *Mutabilitie*, and well it way:
  Me seemes, that though she all unworthy were
  Of the Heav'ns Rule; yet very sooth to say,
  In all things else she beares the greatest sway.
  Which makes me loath this state of life so tickle,
  And love of things so vaine to cast away;
  Whose flowring pride, so fading and so fickle,
Short *Time* shall soon cut down with his consuming sickle.

2

Then gin I thinke on that which Nature said,
  Of that same time when no more *Change* shall be,
  But stedfast rest of all things firmly stayd
  Vpon the pillours of Eternity,
  That is contrayr to *Mutabilitie*:
  For, all that moueth, doth in *Change* delight:
  But thenceforth all shall rest eternally
  With Him that is the God of Sabaoth hight:
O that great Sabaoth God, graunt me that Sabaoths sight.

THE HISTORIE OF THE WORLD

The Preface

How unfit, and how unworthy a choice I have made of my self, to undertake a worke of this mixture; mine owne reason, though exceeding weake, hath sufficiently resolved me. For had it beene begotten then with my first dawne of day, when the light of common knowledge began to open it selfe to my yonger yeares : and before any wound received, either from Fortune or Time: I might yet well have doubted, that the darkenesse of Age and Death would have covered over both It and Mee, long before the performance. For, beginning with the Creation: I have proceeded with the History of the World; and lastly purposed (sone few sallies excepted) to confine my Discourse, with this our renowned Iland of *Great Brittaine*. I confesse that it had better sorted with my dissability, the better part of whose times are run out in other travailles; to have set together (as I could) the unjoynted and scattered frame of our English affaires, than of the universall: in whome had there beene no other defect, (who am all defect) then the time of the day, it were enough; the day of a tempestuous life, drawne on to the very evening ere I began. But those inmost, and soule-peircing wounds, which are ever aking while uncured: with the desire to satisfie those few friends, which I have tried by the fire of adversitie; the former enforcing, the latter perswading; have caused mee to make my thoughts legible, and my selfe the Subject of every opinion wise or weake. . . .

For my selfe, if I have in any thing served my Country, and prised it before my private: the generall acceptation can yeeld me no other profit at this time, than doth a faire sunshine day to a Sea-man after shipwrack; and the contrary no other harme than an out-ragious tempest after the port attained. I know that I lost the love of many, for my fidelity towardes Her, whom I must still honor in the dust; though further than the defence of Her excellent person,

I never persequuted any man. Of those that did it, and by what device they did it: He that is the Supreame Judge of all the world, hath taken the accompt; so as for this kind of suffering, I must say with *Seneca, Mala opinio, benè parta, delectat.* . . .

To me it belongs in the first part of this prefæce, following the common and approved custome of those who have left the memories of time past to after ages; to give, as neare as I can, the same right to History which they have done. Yet seeing therein I should but borrow other mens wordes; I will not trouble the Reader with the repetition. . . . And it is not the least debt which we owe unto History, that it hath made us acquainted with our dead Ancestors; and, out of the depth and darkenesse of the earth, delivered us their memory and fame. In a word, we may gather out of History a policy no lesse wise than eternall; by the comparison and application of other mens fore-passed miseries, with our owne like errours and ill deservings.

But it is neither of Examples the most lively instructions, nor the words of the wisest men, nor the terror of future torments, that hath yet so wrought in our blind and stupified mindes; as to make us remember, That the infinite eye and wisdome of GOD doth peirce through all our pretences; as to make us remember, That the justice of GOD doth require none other accuser, than our owne consciences: which neither the false beauty of our apparent actions, nor all the formallitie, which (to pacifie the opinions of men) we put on; can in any, or the least kind, cover from his knowledge. And so much did that Heathen wisdome confesse, no way as yet qualified by the knowledge of a true GOD. If any (saith Eurypides) *having in his life committed wickednesse, thinke hee can hide it from the everlasting gods, he thinkes not well.*

To repeat GODS judgements in particular, upon those of all degrees, which have plaied with his mercies; would require a volume apart: for the *Sea* of examples hath no bottome. The markes, set on private men, are with their bodies cast into the earth; and their fortunes, written onely in the memories of those that lived with them: so as they who succeed, and have not seene the fall of others, doe not feare their owne faults. GODS judgments upon the greater and greatest, have beene left to posterity; first, by those happy hands which the Holy Ghost hath guided; and secondly, by their vertue, who have gathered the acts and ends of men, mighty and remarkeable in the world. Now to poynt farre off, and to speake of the conversion of Angells into Deuills, for Ambition: Or of the greatest and most glorious Kings, who have gnawne the grasse of the earth with beasts, for pride and ingratitude towards GOD: Or of that wise working of *Pharao*, when he slue the Infants of *Israel*, ere they had recovered their Cradles: Or of the policy of *Jezabel* in covering the murder of *Naboth* by a triall of the *Elders*, according to the Law: with many thousands of the like: what were it other, than to make an hopelesse proofe, that farre-off examples would not be left to the same farre-off respects, as heretofore? For who hath not observed, what labour, practise, perill, bloudshed, and cruelty, the Kings and Princes of the world have undergone, exercised, taken on them, and committed; to make them-selves and their issues maisters of the world? And yet hath *Babylon, Persia, Egypt, Syria, Macedon, Carthage, Rome*, and the rest, no fruit, no flower, grasse, nor leafe, springing upon the face of the Earth, of those seedes: No; their very roots and ruines doe hardly remaine. *Omnia quae manu hominum facta sunt, vel manu hominum evertuntur, vel stando & durando deficiunt: All that the hand of man can make is either over-turnd by the hand of man, or at length by standing and continuing consumed.* The reasons of whose ruines, are diversly given by those that ground their opinions on second causes. All Kingdomes and States have fallen (say the Politicians) by outward and forraine force, or by inward negligence and dissension, or by a third cause arising from both: Others observe, That the greatest have sunck downe under their owne weight; of which *Livie* hath a touch: *eo crevit, ut magnitudine laboret sua*: Others, That the divine providence (which *Cratippus* objected to *Pompey*) hath set downe the date and period of every estate, before their first foundation and erection. But hereof I will give my selfe a day over to resolve. . . .

Oh by what plots, by what forswearings, betrayings, oppressions, imprisonments, tortures, poysonings, and under what reasons of State, and politique subteltie, have these forenamed Kings, both strangers, and of our owne Nation, pulled the vengeance of GOD upon them-selves, upon theirs, and upon their prudent ministers!

and in the end have brought those things to passe for their enemies, and seene an effect so directly contrarie to all their owne counsailles and cruelties; as the one could never have hoped for themselves; and the other never have succeeded; if no such opposition had ever beene made. GOD hath said it and performed it ever: *Perdam sapientiam sapientum, I will destroy the wisdome of the wise.*

But what of all this? and to what end doe we lay before the eies of the living, the fal and fortunes of the dead: seeing the world is the same that it hath bin; and the children of the present time, wil stil obey their parents? It is in the present time, that all the wits of the world are exercised. To hold the times we have, we hold all things lawfull: and either we hope to hold them for ever; or at least we hope, that there is nothing after them to bee hoped for. For as wee are content to forget our owne experience, and to counterfeit the ignorance of our owne knowledge, in all things that concerne our selves; or perswade our selves, that GOD hath given us letters patents to pursue all our irreligious affections, with a *non obstante*: so wee neither looke behind us what hath beene, nor before us what shall bee. It is true, that the quantitie which wee have, is of the body: wee are by it joyned to the earth: we are compounded of earth; and wee inhabite it. The Heavens are high, farr off, and unsearcheable: wee have sense and feeling of corporal things; and of eternall grace, but by revelation. No mervaille then that our thoughts are also earthlie: and it is lesse to be wondred at, that the words of worthlesse men cannot cleanse them: seeing their doctrine and instruction, whose understanding the Holy Ghost vouchsafed to inhabite, have not performed it. For as the Prophet *Esai* cryed out long agone, *Lord, who hath beleeved our reports?* And out of doubt, as *Esai* complained then for him selfe and others: so are they lesse beleeved, every day after other. For although Religion, and the truth thereof, bee in every mans mouth, yea in the discourse of every woman, who for the greatest number are but *Idolls of vanitie*: what is it other than an universall dissimulation?[1] Wee professe that wee know GOD: but by workes we deny him. For Beatitude doth not consist in the knowledge of divine things, but in a divine life: for the Devills know them better than men. *Beatitudo non est*

[1] *Paule to Titus, Ch. 1, ve. 10.*

46

divinorum cognitio, sed vita divina. And certainly there is nothing more to bee admired, and more to bee lamented, than the privat contention, the passionate dispute, the personall hatred, and the perpetuall warre, massacres, and murders, for Religion among *Christians*: the discourse whereof hath so occupied the World, as it hath well neare driven the practise thereof out of the world. . . . Wee are all (in effect) become Comaedians in religion: and while we act in gesture and voice, divine vertues, in all the course of our lives wee renounce our Persons, and the parts wee play. For Charitie, Justice, and Truth, have but their being *in termes*, like the Philosophers *Materia prima.*

Neither is it that wisedome, which *Salomon* defineth to be the *Schoole-Mistresse of the knowledge of* GOD, that hath valuation in the world: it is enough that we give it our good word; but the same which is altogether exercised in the service of the World, as the gathering of riches cheifly; by which we purchase and obtaine honour, with the many respects which attend it. . . .

But let every man value his owne wisdome, as hee pleaseth. Let the Rich man thinke all fooles, that cannot equall his aboundance; the Revenger esteeme all negligent, that have not troden down their opposites; the Politician, all grosse, that cannot merchandize their faith: Yet when we once come in sight of the Port of death, to which all winds drive us, and when by letting fall that fatall Anchor, which can never be weighed again, the Navigation of this life takes end: Then it is I say, that our owne cogitations (those sad and severe cogitations, formerly beaten from us by our Health and Felicitie) returne againe, and pay us to the uttermost for all the pleasing passages of our lives past. It is then that wee crie out to GOD for mercie; then, when our selves can no longer exercise cruelty towards others: and it is onely then, that wee are strucken through the soule with this terrible sentence, *That* GOD *will not be mockt.*[1] For if according to Saint *Peter*,[2] *The righteous scarcely bee saved: and that* GOD *spared not his Angells:* where shall those appeare, who, having served their appetites all their lives presume to thinke, that the severe commandements of the All-powerfull GOD were given but in sport; and that the short breath, which wee draw when death

[1] Galat. 6. 7.   [2] Pet. 1. 4 [18].

47

presseth us, if wee can but fashion it to the sound of *Mercy* (without any kinde of satisfaction or amends) is sufficient? *O quam multi*, saith a reverend Father, *Cum hac spe ad æternos labores & bella descendunt*: I confesse that it is a great comfort to our friends, to have it said, that wee ended wel; for wee all desire (as *Balaam* did) *to die the death of the righteous*. But what shall wee call a disesteeming, an apposing, or (indeed) a mocking of GOD; if those men doe not appose him, disesteeme him, and mocke him, that thinke it enough for GOD, to aske him forgivenesse at leisure, with the remainder and last drawing of a malitious breath? . . .

. . . For what-so-ever is cast behind us, is just nothing: and what is to come, deceiptfull hope hath it: *Omnia quæ eventura sunt, in incerto iacent*. Onely those few blacke Swannes I must except: who having had the grace to value worldly vanities at no more than their owne price; doe, by retayning the comfortable memorie of a well acted life, behold death without dread, and the grave without feare; and embrace both, as necessary guides to endlesse glorie.

For my selfe, this is my consolation, and all that I can offer to others, that the sorrowes of this life, are but of two sorts: whereof the one hath respect to GOD; the other, to the World. In the first wee complaine to GOD against our selves, for our offences against him; and confesse, *Et tu iustus es in omnibus quæ venerunt super nos, And thou O Lord art just in all that hath befallen us*. In the second wee complaine to our selves against GOD: as if hee had done us wrong, either in not giving us worldly goods and honours, answering our appetites: or for taking them againe from us, having had them; forgetting that humble and just acknowledgment of *Job*, *The Lord hath given, and the Lord hath taken*. To the first of which Saint *Paul* hath promised blessednesse; to the second, death. And out of doubt hee is either a foole or ungratefull to GOD, or both, that doth not acknowledge, how meane so-ever his estate bee, that the same is yet farre greater, than that which GOD oweth him: or doth not acknowledge, how sharpe so-ever his afflictions bee, that the same are yet farre lesse, than those which are due unto him. And if an Heathen wise man call the adversities of the world but *tributa vivendi*, *the tributes of living*: a wise Christian man ought to know them, and beare them, but as the tributes of offending. He ought to beare them man-like, and resolvedly; and not as those whining souldiors do, *qui gementes sequuntur imperatorem.*

For seeing God, who is the Author of all our tragedies, hath written out for us, and appointed us all the parts we are to play: and hath not, in their distribution, beene partiall to the most mighty Princes of the world; That gave unto *Darius* the part of the greatest Emperour, and the part of the most miserable begger, a begger begging water of an Enemie, to quench the great drought of death; That appointed *Bajazet* to play the *Gran Signior* of the *Turkes* in the morning, and in the same day the *Footstoole* of *Tamerlane* (both which parts *Valerian* had also playd, beeing taken by *Sapores*) that made *Bellisarius* play the most victorious Captaine, and lastly the part of a blinde beggar; of which examples many thousands may be produced: why should other men, who are but of the least wormes, complaine of wrongs? Certainly there is no other account to be made of this ridiculous world, than to resolve, That the change of fortune on the great Theater, is but as the change of garments on the lesse. For when on the one and the other, every man weares but his own skin; the Players are all alike. Now if any man, out of weaknes, prise the passages of this world otherwise (for saith *Petrarch, Magni ingenii est revocare mentem a sensibus*) it is by reason of that unhappie fantasie of ours, which forgeth in the braines of Man all the miseries (the corporall excepted) whereunto hee is subject: Therein it is, that Misfortune and Adversitie worke all that they worke. For seeing Death, in the end of the Play, takes from all, whatsoever Fortune or Force takes from any one: it were a foolish madnes in the shipwracke of worldly things, where all sinkes but the Sorrow, to save it. That were, as *Seneca* saith, *Fortunæ succumbere, quod tristius est omni fato, To fall under Fortune, of all other the most miserable destinie.* But it is now time to sound a retrait.

. . . If the Phrase be weake, and the Stile not everywhere like it selfe: the first, shews their legitimation and true Parent; the second, will excuse it selfe upon the Variety of Matter. For *Virgill,* who wrote his *Eclogues, gracili avena,* used stronger pipes when he sounded the warres of *Æneas.* It may also bee layd to my charge that I use divers *Hebrew* words in my first booke, and else where:

in which language others may thinke, and I myselfe acknowledge
it, that I am altogether ignorant: but it is true, that some of them
I find in *Montanus*, others in lattaine Carecter in S. *Senensis*, and
of the rest I have borrowed the interpretation of some of my learned
friends.   But say I had beene beholding to neither, yet were it not
to bee wondred at, having had an eleven yeares leasure, to attaine the
knowledge of that, or of any other tongue; How-so-ever, I know
that it will bee said by many, That I might have beene more pleasing
to the Reader, if I had written the Story of mine owne times; having
been permitted to draw water as neare the Well-head as another.
To this I answer, that who-so-ever in writing a moderne Historie,
shall follow truth too neare the heeles, it may happily strike out his
teeth.   There is no Mistresse or Guide, that hath led her followers
and servants into greater miseries.   He that goes after her too farre
off, looseth her sight, and looseth himselfe: and hee that walkes after
her at a middle distance; I know not whether I should call that kinde
of course Temper or Basenesse.   It is true, that I never travailed
after mens opinions, when I might have made the best use of them:
and I have now too few daies remayning, to imitate those, that
either out of extreame ambition, or extreame cowardise, or both,
doe yet, (when death hath them on his shoulders) flatter the world,
between the bed and the grave.   It is enough for me (being in that
state I am) to write of the eldest times: wherein also why may it
not be said, that in speaking of the past, I point at the present, and
taxe the vices of those that are yet lyving, in their persons that are
long since dead; and have it laid to my charge?   But this I cannot
helpe, though innocent.   And certainly if there be any, that finding
themselves spotted like the Tigers of old time, shal finde fault with
me for painting them over a new; they shall therein accuse themselves justly, and me falsely.

For I protest before the Majesty of God, That I malice no man
under the Sunne.   Impossible I know it is to please all: seeing few
or none are so pleased with themselves, or so assured of themselves,
by reason of their subjection to their private passions; but that they
seeme diverse persons in one and the same day.   *Seneca* hath said it,
and so do I: *Unus mihi pro populo erat*: and to the same effect
Epicurus, Hoc ego non multis sed tibi; or (as it hath since lamentably

fallen out) I may borrow the resolution of an ancient Philosopher, *Satis est unus, Satis est nullus.* For it was for the service of that inestimable Prince *Henry,* the successive hope, and one of the greatest of the Christian World, that I undertooke this Worke. It pleased him to peruse some part thereof, and to pardon what was amisse. It is now left to the world without a Maister: from which all that is presented, hath received both blows and thanks. *Eadem probamus, eadem reprehendimus: hic exitus est omnis iudicii, in quo lis secundum plures datur.* But these discourses are idle. I know that as the charitable will judge charitably: so against those, *qui gloriantur in malitia,* my present adversitie hath disarmed mee. I am on the ground already; and therefore have not farre to fall: and for rysing againe, as in the Naturall privation there is no recession to habit; so it is seldome seene in the privation politique. I doe therefore for-beare to stile my Readers *Gentle, Courteous,* and *Friendly,* thereby to beg their good opinions, or to promise a second and third volume (which I also intend) if the first receive grace and good acceptance. For that which is already done, may be thought enough; and too much: and it is certaine, let us claw the Reader with never so many courteous phrases; yet shall we ever-more be thought fooles, that write foolishly. For conclusion; all the hope I have lies in this, That I have already found more ungentle and uncourteous Readers of my Love towards them, and well-deserving of them, than ever I shall doe again. For had it beene otherwise, I should hardly have had this leisure, to have made my selfe a foole in print.

JOHN DONNE

BIATHANATOS

A DECLARATION
OF THAT PARADOXE OR THESIS

That *Self-Homicide* is not so Naturally Sinne that it
may never be otherwise. *Wherein* The Nature, and the
extent of all those Lawes, which seem to be violated
by this Act, are diligently surveyed

1644

The Preface

Declaring the Reasons, the Purpose, the Way, and the End of the AUTHOR

BEZA, A man as eminent and illustrious, in the full glory and Noone
of Learning, as others were in the dawning, and Morning, when any,
the least sparkle was notorious, confesseth of himself, that only for
the anguish of a Scurffe, which over-ranne his head, he had once
drown'd himselfe from the Millers bridge in Paris, if his Uncle by
chance had not then come that way; I have often such a sickly
inclination. And, whether it be, because I had my first breeding
and conversation with men of a suppressed and afflicted Religion,
accustomed to the despite of death, and hungry of an imagin'd
Martyrdome; Or that the common Enemie find that doore worst
locked against him in mee; Or that there bee a perplexitie and
flexibility in the doctrine it selfe; Or because my Conscience ever
assures me, that no rebellious grudging at Gods gifts, nor other sin-
full concurrence accompanies these thoughts in me, or that a brave
scorn, or that a faint cowardlinesse beget it, whensoever any affliction
assails me, me thinks I have the keyes of my prison in mine owne
hand, and no remedy presents it selfe so soon to my heart, as mine
own sword. Often Meditation of this hath wonne me to a charitable interpretation of their action, who dy so: and provoked me a
little to watch and exagitate their reasons, which pronounce so
peremptory judgement upon them.

A devout and godly man, hath guided us well, and rectified our uncharitablenesse in such cases, by this remembrance *Scis lapsum &c. Thou knowest this mans fall, but thou knowest not his wrastling; which perchance was such, that almost his very fall is justified and accepted of God.* For, to this end, saith one, *God hath appointed us tentations, that we might have some excuses for our sinnes, when he calles us to account.*

An uncharitable misinterpreter unthriftily demolishes his own house, and repairs not another. He loseth without any gaine or profit to any. And, as *Tertullian* comparing and making equall, him which provokes another, and him who will be provoked by another, sayes, *There is no difference, but that the provoker offended first, And this is nothing, because in evill there is no respect of Order or Prioritie.* So wee may soone become as ill as any offendor, if we offend in a severe increpation of the fact. For, *Climachus* in his *Ladder of Paradise*, places these two steps very neere one another, when hee sayes, *Though in the world it were possible for thee, to escape all defiling by actuall sinne, yet by judging and condemning those who are defiled, thou art defiled.* In this thou art defiled, as *Basil* notes, *That in comparing others sinnes, thou canst not avoid excusing thine owne.* Especially this is done, if thy zeale be too fervent in the reprehension of others: For, as in most other Accidents, so in this also, Sinne hath the nature of Poyson, that *It enters easiest, and works fastest upon cholerique constitutions.* It is good counsell of the Pharises stiled, *Ne judices proximum donec ad ejus locum pertingas.* Feele and wrastle with such tentations as he hath done, and thy zeale will be tamer. For, *Therefore* (saith the Apostle) *it became Christ to be like us, that he might be mercifull.*

If therefore after a Christian protestation of an innocent purpose herein, And after a submission of all which is said, not only to every Christian Church, but to every Christian man, and after an entreaty, that the Reader will follow this advise of *Tabaeus: Qui litigant, sint ambo in conspectu tuo mali et rei,* and trust neither me, nor the adverse part, but the Reasons, there be any scandall in this enterprise of mine, it is Taken, not Given. And though I know, that the malitious prejudged man, and the lazy affectors of ignorance, will use the same calumnies and obtrectations towards me, (for the voyce and sound of the Snake and Goose is all one) yet because I thought, that as in the poole of *Bethsaida*, there was no health till the water was troubled, so the best way to finde the truth in this matter was to debate and vexe it, (for *We must as well dispute* de veritate, *as* pro veritate,) I abstained not for fear of mis-interpretation from this undertaking. Our stomachs are not now so tender, and queasie, after so long feeding upon solid Divinitie, nor we so umbragious and startling, having been so long enlightened in Gods path, that wee should thinke any truth strange to us, or relapse into that childish age, in which a Councell in *France* forbad *Aristotles Metaphysiques*, and punished with Excommunication the excribing, reading, or having that booke.

Contemplative and bookish men, must of necessitie be more quarrelsome then others, because they contend not about matter of fact, nor can determine their controversies by any certaine witnesses, nor judges. But as long as they goe towards peace, that is Truth, it is no matter which way. The tutelare Angels resisted one another in *Persia*, but neither resisted Gods revealed purpose. *Hierome* and *Gregorie* seem to be of opinion that *Salomon* is damned; *Ambrose* and *Augustine*, that he is saved: All Fathers, all zealous of Gods glorie. At the same time when the *Romane* Church canonized *Becket*, the Schooles of *Paris* disputed whether hee could be saved; both Catholique Judges, and of reverend authoritie. And after so many Ages of a devout and religious celebrating the memory of *Saint Hierome*, *Causaeus* hath spoken so dangerously, that *Campian* saies, hee pronounces him to be as deepe in hell as the Devill. But in all such intricacies, where both opinions seeme equally to conduce to the honor of God, his Justice being as much advanced in the one, as his Mercie in the other, it seemes reasonable to me, that this turne the scales, if on either side there appeare charity towards the poore soule departed. The Church in her Hymnes and Antiphones, doth often salute the Nayles and Crosse, with Epithets of sweetnesse, and thanks; but the Speare which pierced Christ when he was dead, it ever calles, *dirum Mucronem*.

This pietie, I protest again, urges me in this discourse; and what infirmity soever my reasons may have, yet I have comfort in *Trismegistus Axiome*, *Qui pius est, summe Philosophatur*. And therefore without any disguising, or curious and libellous concealing, I present and object it, to all of candour, and indifferencie, to escape that just taxation, *Novum malitiae genus est, et intemperantis, scribere quod occultes.* For as, when *Ladislaus* tooke occasion of the great schisme, to corrupt the Nobility in *Rome*, and hoped thereby to possess the Towne, to their seven Governours whom they called *Sapientes*, they added three more, whom they called *Bonos*, and confided in them; so doe I wish, and as much as I can, effect, that to those many learned and subtile men which have travelled in this point, some charitable and compassionate men might be added.

If therefore of Readers, which *Gorionides* observes to be of foure sorts, (Spunges which attract all without distinguishing; Howre-glasses, which receive and powre out as fast; Bagges, which retaine onely the dregges of the Spices, and let the Wine escape; and Sives which retaine the best onely). I finde some of the last sort, I doubt not but they may bee hereby enlightened. And as the eyes of *Eve* were opened by the taste of the Apple, though it bee said before that shee saw the beauty of the tree, So the digesting of this may bring them to see the nakednesse and deformity of their owne reasons, founded upon a rigorous suspition, and winne them to be of that temper, which *Chrisostome* commends, *He which suspects benignly would faine be deceived, and be overcome, and is piously glad, when he findes it to be false which he did uncharitably suspect.* And it may have as much vigour (as one observes of another Author) as the Sunne in *March*; it may stirre and dissolve humors, though not expell them; for that must bee a worke of a stronger power.

Every branch which is excerpted from other authors, and engrafted here, is not written for the readers faith, but for illustration and comparison. Because I undertooke the declaration of such a proposition as was controverted by many, and therefore was drawn to the citation of many authorities, I was willing to goe all the way with company, and to take light from others, as well in the journey as at the journeys end. If therefore in multiplicity of not necessary citations there appeare vanity, or ostentation, or digression my honesty must make my excuse and compensation, who acknowledge as *Pliny* doth *That to chuse rather to be taken in a theft then to give every man [his] due is* obnoxii animi et infelicis ingenii. I did it the rather because scholastique and artificial men use this way of instructing; and I made account that I was to deale with such, because I presume that naturall men are at least enough inclinable of themselves to this doctrine.

This my way; and my end is to remove scandall. For certainly God often punishes a sinner much more severely, because others have taken occasion of sinning by his fact. If therefore wee did correct in our selves this easiness of being scandalized, how much easier and lighter might we make the punishment of many transgressors? for God in his judgements hath almost made us his assistants, and counsellers, how far he shall punish; and our interpretation of anothers sinne doth often give the measure to Gods Justice or Mercy.

If therefore, since *disorderly long haire which was pride and wantonnesse in* Absolon, *and squallor and horridnes in* Nebuchodonozor, *was vertue and strength in* Samson, *and sanctification in* Samuel, these severe men will not allow to indifferent things the best construction they are capable of, nor pardon my inclination to do so, they shall pardon this opinion, that their severity proceeds from a self-guiltines, and give me leave to apply that of *Ennodius, That it is the nature of stiffe wickednesse, to think that of others which themselves deserve, and it is all the comfort which the guilty have, not to find any innocent.*

JOHN MILTON

THE REASON OF CHURCH GOVERNMENT

1641

Preface to the Second Book

How happy were it for this frail, and as it may be called mortal life
of man, since all earthly things which have the name of good and
convenient in our daily use, are withal so cumbersome and full of
trouble, if knowledge, yet which is the best and lightsomest pos-
session of the mind, were, as the common saying is, no burden; and
that what it wanted of being a load to any part of the body, it did
not with a heavy advantage overlay upon the spirit! For not to
speak of that knowledge that rests in the contemplation of natural
causes and dimensions, which must needs be a lower wisdom, as the
object is low, certain it is, that he who hath obtained in more than
the scantiest measure to know anything distinctly of God, and of
his true worship, and what is infallibly good and happy in the state
of man's life, what in itself evil and miserable, though vulgarly not
so esteemed; he that hath obtained to know this, the only high
valuable wisdom indeed, remembering also that God, even to a
strictness, requires the improvement of these his entrusted gifts,
cannot but sustain a sorer burden of mind, and more pressing than
any supportable toil or weight, which the body can labour under;
how and in what manner he shall dispose and employ those sums
of knowledge and illumination, which God hath sent him into
this world to trade with. And that which aggravates the burden
more, is, that, having received amongst his allotted parcels, certain
precious truths, of such an orient lustre as no diamond can equal;
which nevertheless he has in charge to put off at any cheap rate,
yea, for nothing to them that will; the great merchants of this world,
fearing that this course would soon discover and disgrace the false
glitter of their deceitful wares, wherewith they abuse the people,
like poor Indians with beads and glasses, practise by all means
how they may suppress the vending of such rarities, and at such a

cheapness as would undo them, and turn their trash upon their hands. Therefore by gratifying the corrupt desires of men in fleshly doctrines, they stir them up to persecute with hatred and contempt all those, that seek to bear themselves uprightly in this their spiritual factory: which they foreseeing, though they cannot but testify of truth, and the excellency of that heavenly traffick which they bring, against what opposition or danger soever, yet needs must it sit heavily upon their spirits, that, being in God's prime intention, and their own, selected heralds of peace, and dispensers of treasure inestimable, without price to them that have no peace, they find in the discharge of their commission, that they are made the greatest variance and offence, a very sword and fire both in house and city over the whole earth. This is that which the sad prophet Jeremiah laments: "Wo is me, my mother, that thou hast born me, a man of strife, and contention!" And although divine inspiration must certainly have been sweet to those ancient prophets, yet the irksomeness of that truth which they brought was so unpleasant unto them, that everywhere they call it a burden. Yea, that mysterious book of revelation, which the great evangelist was bid to eat, as it had been some eye-brightening electuary of knowledge and foresight, though it were sweet in his mouth, and in the learning, it was bitter in his belly; bitter in the denouncing. Nor was this hid from the wise poet Sophocles, who in that place of his tragedy, where Tiresias is called to resolve king Œdipus in a matter which he knew would be grievous, brings him in bemoaning his lot, that he knew more than other men. For surely to every good and peaceable man, it must in nature needs be a hateful thing to be a displeaser and molester of thousands; much better would it like him doubtless to be the messenger of gladness and contentment, which is his chief intended business to all mankind, but that they resist and oppose their own true happiness. But when God commands to take the trumpet, and blow a dolorous or a jarring blast, it lies not in man's will what he shall say, or what he shall conceal. If he shall think to be silent, as Jeremiah did, because of the reproach and derision he met with daily, "and all his familiar friends watched for his halting," to be revenged on him for speaking the truth, he would be forced to confess as he confessed; "his word was in my heart as a burning fire shut up in my bones; I was weary with forbearing, and could not stay." Which might teach these times not suddenly to condemn all things that are sharply spoken or vehemently written as proceeding out of stomach, virulence, and ill-nature; but to consider rather, that if the prelates have leave to say the worst that can be said, or do the worst that can be done, while they strive to keep to themselves, to their great pleasure and commodity, those things which they ought to render up, no man can be justly offended with him that shall endeavour to impart and bestow, without any gain to himself, those sharp, but saving words, which would be a terror and a torment in him to keep back. For me, I have determined to lay up as the best treasure and solace of a good old age, if God vouchsafe it me, the honest liberty of free speech from my youth, where I shall think it available in so dear a concernment as the church's good. . . . Concerning therefore this wayward subject against prelaty, the touching whereof is so distasteful and disquietous to a number of men, as by what hath been said I may deserve of charitable readers to be credited, that neither envy nor gall hath entered me upon this controversy, but the enforcement of conscience only, and a preventive fear lest the omitting of this duty should be against me, when I would store up to myself the good provision of peaceful hours: so, lest it should be still imputed to me, as I have found it hath been, that some self-pleasing humour of vain-glory hath incited me to contest with men of high estimation, now while green years are upon my head; from this needless surmisal I shall hope to dissuade the intelligent and equal auditor, if I can but say successfully that which in this exigent behoves me; although I would be heard only, if it might be, by the elegant and learned reader, to whom principally for a while I shall beg leave I may address myself. To him it will be no new thing, though I tell him that if I hunted after praise, by the ostentation of wit and learning, I should not write thus out of mine own season when I have neither yet completed to my mind the full circle of my private studies, although I complain not of any insufficiency to the matter in hand; or were I ready to my wishes, it were a folly to commit any thing elaborately composed to the careless and interrupted listening of these tumultuous times. Next, if I were wise only to my own ends, I would certainly take such a subject as of itself might catch applause, whereas this hath all the disadvantages on the contrary, and such a subject as the publishing whereof might be delayed at pleasure, and time enough to pencil it over with all the curious touches of art, even to the perfection of a faultless picture; whenas in this argument the not deferring is of great moment to the good speeding, that if solidity have leisure to do her office, art cannot have much. Lastly, I should not choose this manner of writing, wherein knowing myself inferior to myself, led by the genial power of nature to another task, I have the use, as I may account, but of my left hand. And though I shall be foolish in saying more to this purpose, yet since it will be such a folly, as wisest men go about to commit, having only confessed and so committed, I may trust with more reason, because with more folly, to have courteous pardon. For although a poet, soaring in the high reason of his fancies, with his garland and singing robes about him, might, without apology, speak more of himself than I mean to do; yet for me sitting here below in the cool element of prose, a mortal thing among many readers of no empyreal conceit, to venture and divulge unusual things of myself, I shall petition to the gentler sort, it may not be envy to me. I must say, therefore, that after I had for my first years, by the ceaseless diligence and care of my father, (whom God recompense!) been exercised to the tongues, and some sciences, as my age would suffer, by sundry masters and teachers both at home and at the schools, it was found, that whether aught was imposed me by them that had the overlooking, or betaken to of mine own choice in English, or other tongue, prosing or versing, but chiefly this latter, the style, by certain vital signs it had, was likely to live. But much latelier in the private academies of Italy, whither I was favoured to resort, perceiving that some trifles which I had in memory, composed at under twenty or thereabout, (for the manner is, that every one must give some proof of his wit and reading there) met with acceptance above what was looked for; and other things, which I had shifted in scarcity of books and convenience to patch up amongst them, were received with written encomiums, which the Italian is not forward to bestow on men of this side the Alps; I began thus far to assent both to them and divers of my friends here at home, and not less to an inward prompting which now grew daily upon me, that by labour and intense study, (which I take to be my portion in this life) joined with the strong propensity of nature, I might perhaps leave something so written to aftertimes, as they should not willingly let it die. These thoughts at once possessed me, and these other; that if I were certain to write as men buy leases, for three lives and downward, there ought no regard be sooner had than to God's glory, by the honour and instruction of my country. For which cause, and not only for that I knew it would be hard to arrive at the second rank among the Latins, I applied myself to that resolution, which Ariosto followed against the persuasions of Bembo, to fix all the industry and art I could unite to the adorning of my native tongue; not to make verbal curiosities the end, (that were a toilsome vanity,) but to be an interpreter and relater of the best and sagest things, among mine own citizens, throughout this island in the mother dialect. That what the greatest and choicest wits of Athens, Rome, or modern Italy, and those Hebrews of old did for their country, I, in my proportion, with this over and above, of being a Christian, might do for mine; not caring to be once named abroad, though perhaps I could attain to that, but content with these British islands as my world; whose fortune hath hitherto been, that if the Athenians, as some say, made their small deeds great and renowned by their eloquent writers, England hath had her noble achievements made small by the unskilful handling of monks and mechanics.

Time serves not now, and perhaps I might seem too profuse to give any certain account of what the mind at home, in the spacious circuits of her musing, hath liberty to propose to herself, though of highest hope and hardest attempting; whether that epic form whereof the two poems of Homer, and those other two of Virgil and Tasso, are a diffuse, and the book of Job a brief model: or whether the rules of Aristotle herein are strictly to be kept, or nature to be followed, which in them that know art, and use judgment, is no transgression, but an enriching of art: and lastly, what king or knight, before the conquest, might be chosen in whom to lay the pattern of a christian hero. And as Tasso gave to a prince of Italy his choice whether he would command him to write of Godfrey's expedition against the Infidels, or Belisarius against the Goths, or Charlemain against the Lombards; if to the instinct of nature and the emboldening of art aught may be trusted, and that there be nothing adverse in our climate, or the fate of this age, it haply would be no rashness, from an equal diligence and inclination, to present the like offer in our own ancient stories; or whether those dramatic constitutions, wherein Sophocles and Euripides reign, shall be found more doctrinal and exemplary to a nation. The Scripture also affords us a divine pastoral drama in the Song of Solomon, consisting of two persons, and a double chorus, as Origen rightly judges. And the Apocalypse of St. John is the majestic image of a high and stately tragedy, shutting up and intermingling her solemn scenes and acts with a sevenfold chorus of hallelujahs and harping symphonies: and this my opinion the grave authority of Pareus, commenting that book, is sufficient to confirm. Or if occasion shall lead, to imitate those magnific odes and hymns, wherein Pindarus and Callimachus are in most things worthy, some others in their frame judicious, in their matter most an end faulty. But those frequent songs throughout the law and prophets beyond all these, not in their divine argument alone, but in the very critical art of composition, may be easily made appear over all the kinds of lyric poesy to be incomparable. These abilities, wheresoever they be found, are the inspired gift of God rarely bestowed, but yet to some (though most abuse) in every nation: and are of power, beside the office of a pulpit, to inbreed and cherish in a great people the seeds of virtue and public civility, to allay the perturbations of the mind, and set the affections in right tune; to celebrate in glorious and lofty hymns the throne and equipage of God's almightiness, and what he works, and what he suffers to be wrought with high providence in his church; to sing victorious agonies of martyrs and saints, the deeds and triumphs of just and pious nations, doing valiantly through faith against the enemies of Christ; to deplore the general relapses of kingdoms and states from justice and God's true worship. Lastly, whatsoever in religion is holy and sublime, in virtue amiable or grave, whatsoever hath passion or admiration in all the changes of that which is called fortune from without, or the wily subleties and refluxes of man's thoughts from within; all these things with a solid and treatable smoothness to paint out and describe. Teaching over the whole book of sanctity and virtue, through all the instances of example, with such delight to those especially of soft and delicious temper, who will not so much as look upon truth herself, unless they see her elegantly dressed; that whereas the paths of honesty and good life appear now rugged and difficult, though they be indeed easy and pleasant, they will then appear to all men both easy and pleasant, though they were rugged and difficult indeed. And what a benefit this would be to our youth and gentry, may be soon guessed by what we know of the corruption and bane, which they suck in daily from the writings and interludes of libidinous and ignorant poetasters, who having scarce ever heard of that which is the main consistence of a true poem, the choice of such persons as they ought to introduce, and what is moral and decent to each one; do for the most part lay up vicious principles in sweet pills to be swallowed down, and make the taste of virtuous documents harsh and sour. But because the spirit of man cannot demean itself lively in this body, without some recreating intermission of labour and serious things, it were happy for the commonwealth, if our magistrates, as in those famous governments of old, would take into their care, not only the deciding of our contentious law cases and brawls, but the managing of our publick sports and festival pastimes, that they might be, not such as were authorised a while since, the provocations of drunkenness and lust, but such as may inure and harden our bodies by martial exercises to all warlike skill and performance; and may civilize, adorn, and make discreet our minds by the learned and affable meeting of frequent academies, and the procurement of wise and artful recitations, sweetened with eloquent and graceful intice-ments to the love and practice of justice, temperance, and fortitude, instructing and bettering the nation at all opportunities, that the call of wisdom and virtue may be heard everywhere, as Solomon saith; "She crieth without, she uttereth her voice in the streets, in the top of high places, in the chief concourse, and in the openings of the gates." Whether this may not be, not only in pulpits, but after another persuasive method, at set and solemn paneguries, in theatres, porches, or what other place or way, may win most upon the people to receive at once both recreation and instruction; let them in authority consult. The thing which I had to say, and those intentions which have lived within me ever since I could conceive myself any thing worth to my country, I return to crave excuse that urgent reason hath plucked from me, by an abortive and foredated discovery. And the accomplishment of them lies not but in a power above man's to promise; but that none hath by more studious ways endeavoured, and with more unwearied spirit that none shall, that I dare almost aver of myself, as far as life and free leisure will extend; and that the land had once enfranchised herself from this impertinent yoke of prelaty, under whose inquisitorious and tyrannical duncery, no free and splendid wit can flourish. Neither do I think it shame to covenant with any knowing reader, that for some few years yet I may go on trust with him toward the payment of what I am now indebted, as being a work not to be raised from the heat of youth, or the vapours of wine; like that which flows at waste from the pen of some vulgar amourist, or the trencher fury of a rhyming parasite; nor to be obtained by the invocation of dame memory and her siren daughters, but by devout prayer to that eternal Spirit, who can enrich with all utterance and knowledge, and sends out his seraphim, with the hallowed fire of his altar, to touch and purify the lips of whom he pleases: to this must be added industrious and select reading, steady observation, insight into all seemly and generous arts and affairs; till which in some measure be compassed, at mine own peril and cost, I refuse not to sustain this expectation from as many as are not loth to hazard so much credulity upon the best pledges that I can give them. Although it nothing content me to have disclosed thus much beforehand, but that I trust hereby to make it manifest with what small willingness I endure to interrupt the pursuit of no less hopes than these, and leave a calm and pleasing solitariness, fed with cheerful and confident thoughts, to embark in a troubled sea of noises and hoarse disputes. . . . But were it the meanest underservice, if God by his secretary conscience enjoin it, it were sad for me if I should draw back; for me especially, now when all men offer their aid to help, ease, and lighten the difficult labours of the church, to whose service, by the intentions of my parents and friends, I was destined of a child, and in mine own resolutions: till coming to some maturity of years, and perceiving what tyranny had invaded the church, that he who would take orders must subscribe slave, and take an oath withal, which, unless he took with a conscience that would retch, he must either straight perjure, or split his faith; I thought it better to prefer a blameless silence before the sacred office of speaking, bought and begun with servitude and forswearing. However thus church-outed by the prelates, hence may appear the right I have to meddle in these matters, as before the necessity and constraint appeared.

JOHN MILTON

PARADISE LOST
1667

I

Prelude to Book III

HAIL holy light, offspring of Heav'n first-born,
Or of the Eternal Coeternal beam
May I express thee unblam'd? since God is light,
And never but in unapproached light
Dwelt from Eternity, dwelt then in thee,
Bright effluence of bright essence increate,
Or hear'st thou rather pure Ethereal stream,
Whose Fountain who shall tell? before the Sun,
Before the Heavens thou wert, and at the voice
Of God, as with a Mantle didst invest
The rising world of waters dark and deep,
Won from the void and formless infinite.
Thee I revisit now with bolder wing,
Escap't the Stygian Pool, though long detain'd
In that obscure sojourn, while in my flight
Through utter and through middle darkness borne,
With other notes than to the Orphean Lyre
I sung of Chaos and Eternal Night,
Taught by the heav'nly Muse to venture down
The dark descent, and up to reascend
Though hard and rare; thee I revisit safe,
And feel thy sovran vital Lamp; but thou
Revisit'st not these eyes, that rowl in vain
To find thy piercing ray, and find no dawn;
So think a drop serene hath quencht thir Orbs,
Or dim suffusion veil'd. Yet not the more
Cease I to wander where the Muses haunt
Clear Spring, or shady Grove, or Sunny Hill,

Smit with the love of sacred song; but chief
Thee Sion and the flow'ry Brooks beneath
That wash thy hallow'd feet, and warbling flow,
Nightly I visit: nor sometimes forget
Those other two equall'd with me in Fate,
So were I equall'd with them in renown,
Blind Thamyris and blind Maeonides,
And Tiresias and Phineus Prophets old:
Then feed on thoughts, that voluntary move
Harmonious numbers; as the wakeful Bird
Sings darkling, and in shadiest Covert hid
Tunes her nocturnal Note.   Thus with the Year
Seasons return, but not to me returns
Day, or the sweet approach of Ev'n or Morn,
Or sight of vernal bloom, or Summer's Rose,
Or flocks, or herds, or human face divine;
But cloud instead, and ever-during dark
Surrounds me, from the cheerful ways of men
Cut off, and for the Book of knowledge fair
Presented with a Universal blanc
Of Nature's works to mee expung'd and ras'd,
And wisdom at one entrance quite shut out.
So much the rather thou Celestial Light
Shine inward, and the mind through all her powers
Irradiate, there plant eyes, all mist from thence
Purge and disperse, that I may see and tell
Of things invisible to mortal sight.

II

Prelude to Book VII

Descend from Heav'n Urania, by that name
If rightly thou art call'd, whose Voice divine
Following, above the Olympian Hill I soar,
Above the flight of Pegasean wing.

The meaning, not the Name I call: for thou
Nor of the Muses nine, nor on the top
Of old Olympus dwell'st, but Heav'nly born,
Before the Hills appear'd, or Fountain flow'd,
Thou with Eternal wisdom didst converse,
Wisdom thy Sister, and with her didst play
In presence of th'Almighty Father, pleas'd
With thy Celestial Song. Up led by thee
Into the Heav'n of Heav'ns I have presum'd,
An Earthly Guest, and drawn Empyreal Air,
Thy temp'ring; with like safety guided down
Return me to my Native Element:
Lest from this flying Steed unrein'd, (as once
Bellerophon, though from a lower Clime)
Dismounted, on th'Aleian Field I fall
Erroneous there to wander and forlorn.
Half yet remains unsung, but narrower bound
Within the visible Diurnal Sphere;
Standing on Earth, not rapt above the Pole,
More safe I sing with mortal voice, unchang'd
To hoarse or mute, though fall'n on evil days,
On evil days though fall'n, and evil tongues;
In darkness, and with dangers compast round,
And solitude; yet not alone, whilst thou
Visit'st my slumbers Nightly, or when Morn
Purples the East: still govern thou my Song,
But drive far off the barbarous dissonance
Of Bacchus and his Revellers, the Race
Of that wild Rout that tore the Thracian Bard
In Rhodope, where Woods and Rocks had Ears
To rapture, till the savage clamour drown'd
Both Harp and Voice; nor could the Muse defend
Her Son. So fail not thou, who thee implores;
For thou art Heav'nly, she an empty dream.

68

III

Prelude to Book IX

No more of talk where God or Angel Guest
With Man, as with his Friend, familiar us'd
To sit indulgent, and with him partake
Rural repast, permitting him the while
Venial discourse unblam'd: I now must change
Those Notes to Tragic; foul distrust, and breach
Disloyal on the part of Man, revolt,
And disobedience: on the part of Heav'n
Now alienated, distance and distaste,
Anger and just rebuke, and judgement giv'n,
That brought into this World a world of woe,
Sin and her shadow Death, and Misery
Death's Harbinger: Sad task, yet argument
Not less but more Heroic than the wrauth
Of stern Achilles on his Foe pursu'd
Thrice Fugitive about Troy Wall; or rage
Of Turnus for Lavinia disespous'd,
Or Neptune's ire or Juno's, that so long
Perplex'd the Greek and Cytherea's Son;
If answerable style I can obtain
Of my Celestial Patroness, who designs
Her nightly visitation unimplor'd,
And dictates to me slumb'ring, or inspires
Easy my unpredimated Verse:
Since first this Subject for Heroic Song
Pleas'd me long choosing, and beginning late;
Not sedulous by Nature to indite
Wars, hitherto the only Argument
Heroic deem'd, chief maistry to dissect
With long and tedious havock fabl'd Knights
In Battles feign'd; the better fortitude
Of Patience and Heroic Martyrdom
Unsung; or to describe Races and Games,

Or tilting Furniture, emblazon'd Shields,
Impreses quaint, Caparisons and Steeds,
Bases and tinsel Trappings, gorgeous Knights.
At Joust and Tourneament; then marshall'd Feast
Serv'd up in Hall with Sewers, and Seneschals;
The skill of Artifice or Office mean,
Not that which justly gives Heroick name
To Person or to Poem. Mee of these
Nor skill'd nor studious, higher Argument
Remains, sufficient of itself to raise
That name, unless an age too late, or cold
Climate, or Years damp my intended wing
Deprest, and much they may, if all be mine,
Not hers who brings it nightly to my Ear.

JOHN DRYDEN

THE TEMPEST

1669

As when a tree's cut down, the secret root
Lives under ground, and thence new branches shoot;
So, from old Shakespeare's honoured dust, this day
Springs up and buds a new-reviving play:
Shakespeare, who (taught by none) did first impart
To Fletcher wit, to labouring Jonson art.
He monarch-like, gave those, his subjects law;
And is that nature which they paint and draw.
Fletcher reached that which on his heights did grow,
Whilst Jonson crept, and gathered all below.
This did his love, and this his mirth digest:
One imitates him most, the other best.
If they have since outwrit all other men,
'Tis with the drops which fell from Shakespeare's pen.
The storm, which vanished on the neighbouring shore,
Was taught by Shakespeare's Tempest first to roar.
That innocence and beauty, which did smile
In Fletcher, grew on this enchanted isle.
But Shakespeare's magic could not copied be;
Within that circle none durst walk but he.
I must confess 'twas bold, nor would you now
That liberty to vulgar wits allow,
Which works by magic supernatural things:
But Shakespeare's power is sacred as a king's.
Those legends from old priesthood were received,
And he then writ as people then believed.

.   .   .   .   .

71

JOHN DRYDEN

CLEOMENES

THE SPARTAN HERO

A Tragedy
1692

To the Right Honourable the Earl of Rochester, K.G. &c.

IT is enough for your lordship to be conscious to yourself of having performed a just and honourable action, in redeeming this play from the persecution of my enemies; but it would be ingratitude in me not to publish it to the world. That it has appeared on the stage, is principally owing to you: that it has succeeded, is the approbation of your judgement by that of the public. It is just the inversion of an Act of Parliament. Your lordship first signed it, and after then it was passed amongst the Lords and Commons. The children of old men are generally observed to be short-lived, and of a weakly constitution. How this may prove, I know not, but hitherto it has promised well; and if it survive to posterity, it will carry the noble fame of its patron along with it; or rather, it will be carried by yours to after ages. Ariosto, in his "Voyage of Astolpho to the Moon," has given us a fine allegory of two swans; who, when Time had thrown the writings of many poets into the river of oblivion, were ever in a readiness to secure the best, and bear them aloft into the temple of immortality. Whether this poem be of that number, is left to the judgement of the swan who has preserved it; and, though I can claim little from his justice, I may presume to value myself upon his charity. It will be told me, that I have mistaken the Italian poet, who means only that some excellent writers, almost as few in number as the swans, have rescued the memory of their patrons from forgetfulness and time; when a vast multitude of crows and vultures, that is, bad scribblers, parasites, and flatterers, oppressed by the weight of the names which they endeavoured to redeem, were forced to let them fall into Lethe, where they were lost for ever. If it be thus, my lord, the table would be turned upon me; but I should only fail in my vain attempt; for, either some immortal swan will be more capable of sustaining such a weight, or you, who have been so long conversant in the management of great affairs, are able with your pen to do justice to yourself, and, at the same time, to give the nation a clearer and more faithful insight into those transactions wherein you have worthily sustained so great a part; for, to your experience in State affairs, you have also joined no vulgar erudition, which all your modesty is not able to conceal: for, to understand critically the delicacies of Horace is a height to which few of our noblemen have arrived; and that this is your deserved commendation, I am a living evidence, as far, at least, as I can be allowed a competent judge on that subject. Your affection to that admirable Ode, which Horace writes to his Maecenas, and which I had the honour to inscribe to you, is not the only proof of this assertion. You may please to remember that, in the late happy conversation which I had with your lordship at a noble relation's of yours, you took me aside, and pleased yourself with repeating to me one of the most beautiful pieces in that author. It was the Ode to Barine, wherein you were so particularly affected with that elegant expression, *Juvenumque prodis publica cura.* There is indeed the virtue of a whole poem in those words; that *curiosa felicitas*, which Petronius so justly ascribes to our author. The barbarity of our language is not able to reach it; yet, when I have leisure, I mean to try how near I can raise my English to his Latin; though in the meantime, I cannot but imagine to myself, with what scorn his sacred *manes* would look on so lame a translation as I could make. His *recalcitrat undique tutus* might more easily be applied to me than he himself applied it to Augustus Caesar. I ought to reckon that day as very fortunate to me, and distinguish it, as the ancients did, with a whiter stone; because it furnished me with an occasion of reading my "Cleomenes" to a beautiful assembly of ladies, where your lordship's three fair daughters were pleased to grace it with their presence; and if I may have leave to single out anyone in particular, there was your admirable daughter-in-law, shining, not like a star, but a constellation of herself, a more true and brighter Berenice. Then it was, that, whether out of your own partiality, and indulgence to my writings, or out of complaisance to the fair company, who gave the first good omen to my success by their approbation, your lordship was pleased to add your own, and afterwards to represent it to the queen, as wholly innocent of those crimes which were laid unjustly to its charge. Neither am I to forget my charming patroness, though she will not allow my public address to her in a dedication, but protects me unseen, like my guardian-angel, and shuns my gratitude, like a fairy, who is bountiful by stealth, and conceals the giver when she bestows the gift; but my Lady Silvius has been juster to me, and pointed out the goddess at whose altar I was to pay my sacrifice and thankoffering; and, had she been silent, yet my Lord Chamberlain himself, in restoring my play without any alteration, avowed to me that I had the most earnest solicitress, as well as the fairest, and that nothing could be refused to my Lady Hyde.

These favours, my lord, received from you and your noble family, have encouraged me to this Dedication; wherein I not only give you back a play, which, had you not redeemed it, had not been mine; but at the same time, dedicate to you the unworthy author, with my inviolable faith, and (how mean soever) my utmost service; and I shall be proud to hold my dependence on you in chief, as I do part of my small fortune in Wiltshire. Your goodness has not been wanting to me during the reign of my two masters; and, even from a bare treasury, my success has been contrary to that of Mr. Cowley; and Gideon's fleece has then been moistened, when all the ground has been dry about it. Such and so many provocations of this nature have concurred to my invading of your modesty with this address. I am sensible that it is in a manner forced upon you; but your lordship has been the aggressor in this quarrel, by so many favours, which you were not weary of conferring on me, though at the same time, I own the ambition on my side to be ever esteemed,

Your lordship's most thankful

And most obedient Servant

John Dryden

GEORGE BERKELEY

PASSIVE OBEDIENCE

Or

THE CHRISTIAN DOCTRINE
OF NOT RESISTING THE SUPREME POWER
PROVED & VINDICATED
VPON THE PRINCIPLES OF THE LAW OF NATURE
IN A DISCOURSE DELIVERED AT THE CHAPEL
OF TRINITY COLLEGE, DUBLIN

Nec vero aut per Senatum aut per Populum solvi hac lege possumus

CICERO: Fragmt. *de Repub.*

To the Reader

THAT an absolute passive obedience ought not to be paid any civil power, but that submission should be measured and limited by the public good of the society; and that therefore subjects may lawfully resist the supreme authority, in those cases where the public good shall plainly seem to require it; nay, that it is their duty to do so, inasmuch as they are all under an indispensible obligation to promote the common interest:—these and the like notions, which I cannot help thinking pernicious to mankind, and repugnant to right reason having of late years been industriously cultivated, and set in the most advantageous lights by men of parts and learning, it seemed necessary to arm the youth of our University against them, and take care they go into the world well-principled:—I do not mean obstinately prejudiced in favour of a party, but, from an early acquaintance with their duty, and the clear rational grounds of it, determined to such practices as may speak them good Christians and loyal subjects.

In this view, I made three discourses not many months since in the College-chapel, which some who heard thought it might be of use to make more public; and indeed the false accounts that are gone abroad concerning them have made it necessary.[1] Accordingly

[1] Berkeley laid himself open by this sermon to the charge of being a Jacobite; but this was not his intention.   He was a loyal Hanoverian.

I now send them into the world under the form of one entire Discourse.

To conclude, as in writing these thoughts it was my endeavour to preserve that cool and impartial temper which becomes every sincere inquirer after truth, so I heartily wish they may be read with the same disposition. (1713)

What Berkeley undertakes to defend is the principle of passive obedience, that rebellion is a sin. He is as always determined to identify Christian moral teaching with the demands of right reason. Waiving all appeal to Scripture, he develops what has been called a "theological utilitarianism." All men desire happiness, and by their bearing on happiness denominate things as *good* or *evil*. Now as God is a being of infinite goodness, the end He proposes in all His commands must be good. "But, God enjoying in Himself all possible perfection, it follows that the end is not His own good but that of His creatures," of all without respect to persons. Whatever, therefore, we see clearly to be for the good of all men must be the will of God, and it is as such that it is to us a duty. But how are we to know what is thus good for all men? There are, he says, two ways. The one is that which Godwin later adopted. In every set of circumstances the individual can by thought see what is the best line of conduct. This Berkeley rejects as impossible. The other is to be guided by "the observation of certain universal, determinate rules or moral precepts which in their own nature have a necessary tendency to promote the wellbeing of the sum of mankind in all nations and ages." Such are called *laws of nature* . . . are said to be *stamped on the mind*, to be *engraven on the tables of the heart*. . . . Lastly they are termed *eternal rules of reason* "because they necessarily result from the nature of things and may be demonstrated by the infallible deductions of reason." Examples are "Thou shalt not forswear thyself," "Thou shalt not steal," etc., and it is among these that he places the rule of obedience to established government. There was no more independent, personal thinker in the century, none who so combined profound insight with real or apparent paradox; and no finer character.

HENRY FIELDING

TOM JONES

Prelude to Book VI—of Love

In our last book we have been obliged to deal pretty much with the passion of love; and in our succeeding book, shall be forced to handle this subject still more largely. It may not, therefore, in this place, be improper to apply ourselves to the examination of that modern doctrine, by which certain philosophers, among many other wonderful discoveries, pretend to have found out, that there is no such passion in the human breast.

Whether these philosophers be the same with that surprising sect, who are honourably mentioned by the late Dr. Swift; as having, by the mere force of genius alone, without the least assistance of any kind of learning, or even reading, discovered that profound and invaluable secret, that there was no God: or whether they are not rather the same with those who, some years since, very much alarmed the world, by showing that there were no such things as virtue or goodness really existing in human nature, and who deduced our best actions from pride, I will not here presume to determine. In reality, I am inclined to suspect, that all these several finders of truth are the very identical men, who are by others called the finders of gold. The method used in both these searches after truth and gold, being indeed, one and the same; viz. the searching, rummaging, and examining into a nasty place; indeed in the former instances, into the nastiest of all places, *a bad mind*.

But though, in this particular, and perhaps in their success, the truth-finder and the gold-finder, may very properly be compared together; yet in modesty, surely there can be no comparison between the two; for who ever heard of a gold-finder that had the impudence or folly to assert, from the ill success of his search, that there was no such thing as gold in the world? Whereas the truth-finder, having raked out that jakes, his own mind, and being there capable of tracing no ray of divinity, nor any thing virtuous, or good, or

77

lovely or loving, very fairly, honestly, and logically concludes, that no such things exist in the whole creation. To avoid, however, all contention, if possible, with these philosophers, if they will be called so; and to show our own disposition to accommodate matters peaceably between us, we shall here make some concessions, which may possibly put an end to the dispute.

First, we will grant that many minds, and perhaps those of the philosophers, are entirely free from the least traces of such a passion.

Secondly, that what is commonly called love, namely, the desire of satisfying a voracious appetite with a certain quantity of delicate white human flesh, is by no means that passion for which I here contend. This is indeed more properly hunger; and as no glutton is ashamed to apply the word love to his appetite, and to say he *loves* such and such dishes, so may the lover of this kind, with equal propriety say, he *hungers* after such and such women.

Thirdly, I will grant, which I believe will be a most acceptable concession, that this love for which I am an advocate, though it satisfies itself in a much more delicate manner, doth nevertheless seek its own satisfaction as much as the grossest of all our appetites.

And, lastly, that this love, when it operates towards one of a different sex, is very apt, towards its complete gratification, to call in the aid of that hunger which I have mentioned above; and which it is so far from abating, that it heightens all its delights to a degree scarce imaginable by those who have never been susceptible of any other emotions, than what have proceeded from appetite alone.

In return to all these concessions, I desire of the philosophers to grant that there is in some (I believe in many) human breasts, a kind and benevolent disposition, which is gratified by contributing to the happiness of others. That in this gratification alone, as in friendship, in parental and filial affection, and indeed in general philanthropy, there is a great and exquisite delight. That if we will not call such disposition love, we have no name for it. That though the pleasure arising from such pure love may be heightened and sweetened by the assistance of amorous desires, yet the former can subsist alone, nor are they destroyed by the intervention of the latter. Lastly, that esteem and gratitude are the proper motives to love, as youth and beauty are to desire; and therefore though such desire may naturally cease, when age or sickness overtakes its object, yet these can have no effect on love, nor ever shake or remove, from a good mind, that sensation or passion which hath gratitude and esteem for its basis.

To deny the existence of a passion, of which we often see manifest instances, seems to be very strange and absurd; and can indeed proceed only from that self-admonition which we have mentioned above: but how unfair is this. Doth the man who recognises in his own heart no traces of avarice or ambition conclude, therefore, that there are no such passions in human nature? Why will we not modestly observe the same rule in judging of the good, as well as the evil of others? Or why, in any case, will we, as Shakespeare phrases it, "put the world in our own person?"

Predominant vanity is, I am afraid, too much concerned here. This is one instance of that adulation which we bestow on our own minds, and this almost universally. For there is scarce any man, how much soever he may despise the character of a flatterer, but will condescend in the meanest manner to flatter himself.

To those, therefore, I apply for the truth of the above observations, whose own minds can bear testimony to what I have advanced.

Examine your heart, my good reader, and resolve whether you do believe these matters with me. If you do, you may now proceed to their exemplification in the following pages; if you do not, you have, I assure you, already read more than you have understood; and it would be wiser to pursue business, or your pleasures (such as they are), than to throw away any more of your time in reading what you can neither taste nor comprehend. To treat of the effects of love to you must be as absurd as to discourse on colours to a man born blind; since possibly your idea of love may be as absurd as that which we are told such blind man once entertained of the colour red: that colour seemed to him to be very much like the sound of a trumpet; and love probably may, in your opinion, very greatly resemble a dish of soup, or a sirloin of roast-beef.

SAMUEL JOHNSON

A DICTIONARY
OF THE ENGLISH LANGUAGE
1755

Preface

IT is the fate of those who toil at the lower employments of life, to be rather driven by the fear of evil, than attracted by the prospect of good; to be exposed to censure, without hope of praise; to be disgraced by miscarriage, or punished for neglect, where success would have been without applause, and diligence without reward.

Among these unhappy mortals is the writer of dictionaries; whom mankind have considered, not as the pupil, but the slave of science, the pioneer of literature, doomed only to remove rubbish and clear obstructions from the paths through which Learning and Genius press forward to conquest and glory, without bestowing a smile on the humble drudge that facilitates their progress. Every other author may aspire to praise; the lexicographer can only hope to escape reproach, and even this negative recompense has been yet granted to very few.

I have, notwithstanding this discouragement, attempted a Dictionary of the English Language, which, while it was employed in the cultivation of every species of literature, has itself been hitherto neglected; suffered to spread under the direction of chance, into wild exuberance; resigned to the tyranny of time and fashion; and exposed to the corruptions of ignorance and caprices of innovation.

When I took the first survey of my undertaking, I found our speech copious without order, and energetic without rule; wherever I turned my view, there was perplexity to be disentangled and confusion to be regulated; choice was to be made out of boundless variety, without any established principle of selection; adulterations were to be detected, without a settled test of purity; and modes of expression to be rejected or received, without the suffrages of any writers of classical reputation or acknowledged authority.

Having therefore no assistance but from general grammar, I applied myself to the perusal of our writers; and noting whatever might be of use to ascertain or illustrate any word or phrase, accumulated in time the materials of a dictionary, which, by degrees, I reduced to method, establishing to myself, in the progress of the work, such rules as experience and analogy suggested to me; experience, which practice and observation were continually increasing; and analogy, which, though in some words obscure, was evident in others.

In adjusting the *Orthography*, which has been to this time unsettled and fortuitous, I found it necessary to distinguish those irregularities that are inherent in our tongue, and perhaps coeval with it, from others which the ignorance or negligence of later writers has produced. . . .

In this part of the work, where caprice has long wantoned without control, and vanity sought praise by petty reformation, I have endeavoured to proceed with a scholar's reverence for antiquity, and a grammarian's regard to the genius of our tongue. I have attempted few alterations, and among those few, perhaps the greater part is from the modern to the ancient practice; and I hope I may be allowed to recommend to those, whose thoughts have been perhaps employed too anxiously on verbal singularities, not to disturb, upon narrow views, or for minute propriety, the orthography of their fathers. It has been asserted, that for the law to be *known*, is of more importance than to be *right*. "Change," says Hooker, "is not made without inconvenience, even from worse to better." There is in constancy and stability a general and lasting advantage, which will always overbalance the slow improvements of gradual correction. Much less ought our written language to comply with the corruptions of oral utterance, or copy that which every variation of time or place makes different from itself, and imitate those changes, which will again be changed, while imitation is employed in observing them.

This recommendation of steadiness and uniformity does not proceed from an opinion that particular combinations of letters have much influence on human happiness; or that truth may not be successfully taught by modes of spelling fanciful and erroneous; I am not yet so lost in lexicography as to forget that *words are the daughters of earth, and that things are the sons of heaven.* Language is only the instrument of science, and words are but the signs of ideas; I wish, however, that the instrument might be less apt to decay, and that signs might be permanent, like the things which they denote. . . .

That part of my work, on which I expect malignity most frequently to fasten, is the *explanation*; in which I cannot hope to satisfy those, who are perhaps not inclined to be pleased, since I have not always been able to satisfy myself. To interpret a language by itself, is very difficult; many words cannot be explained by synonimes, because the idea signified by them has not more than one appellation; nor by paraphrase, because simple ideas cannot be described. When the nature of things is unknown, or the notion unsettled and indefinite, and various in various minds, the words by which such notions are conveyed, or such things denoted, will be ambiguous and perplexed. And such is the fate of hapless lexicography, that not only darkness, but light, impedes and distresses it; things may be not only too little, but too much known, to be happily illustrated. To explain, requires the use of terms less abstruse than that which is to be explained, and such terms cannot always be found; for as nothing can be proved but by supposing something intuitively known, and evident without proof, so nothing can be defined but by the use of words too plain to admit a definition.

Other words there are, of which the sense is too subtle and evanescent to be fixed in a paraphrase; such are all those which are by the grammarians termed expletives, and in dead languages are suffered to pass for empty sounds, of no other use than to fill a verse, or to modulate a period, but which are easily perceived in living tongues to have power and emphasis, though it be sometimes such as no other form of expression can convey.

My labour has likewise been much increased by a class of verbs too frequent in the English language, of which the signification is so loose and general, the use so vague and indeterminate, and the senses detorted so widely from the first idea, that it is hard to trace them through the maze of variation, to catch them on the brink of utter inanity, to circumscribe them by any limitations, or interpret them by any words of distinct and settled meaning; such are *bear*, *break*, *come*, *cast*, *full*, *get*, *give*, *do*, *put*, *set*, *go*, *run*, *make*, *take*, *turn*, *throw*. If of these the whole power is not accurately delivered, it must be remembered, that while our language is yet living, and variable by the caprice of every one that speaks it, these words are hourly shifting their relations, and can no more be ascertained in a dictionary, than a grove, in the agitation of a storm, can be accurately delineated from its picture in the water.

The particles are among all nations applied with so great latitude, that they are not easily reducible under any regular scheme of explication; this difficulty is not less, nor perhaps greater in English, than in other languages. I have laboured them with diligence, I hope with success; such at least as can be expected in a task, which no man, however learned or sagacious, has yet been able to perform.

Some words there are which I cannot explain, because I do not understand them; these might have been omitted very often with little inconvenience, but I would not so far indulge my vanity as to decline this confession; for when Tully owns himself ignorant whether *lessus*, in the twelve tables, means a *funeral song* or *mourning garment*; and Aristotle doubts whether οὔρευς in the Iliad signifies a *mule* or *muleteer*, I may surely, without shame, leave some obscurities to happier industry, or future information.

The rigour of interpretative lexicography requires that *the explanation* and *the word explained should be always reciprocal*; this I have always endeavoured, but could not always attain. Words are seldom exactly synonimous; a new term was not introduced, but because the former was thought inadequate; names, therefore, have often many ideas, but few ideas have many names. It was then necessary to use the proximate word, for the deficiency of single terms can very seldom be supplied by circumlocution; nor is the inconvenience great of such mutilated interpretation, because the sense may easily be collected entire from the examples.

In every word of extensive use, it was requisite to mark the progress of its meaning, and show by what gradations of intermediate sense it has passed from its primitive to its remote and accidental signification; so that every foregoing explanation should tend to that which follows, and the series be regularly concatenated from the first notion to the last.

This is specious, but not always practicable; kindred senses may be so interwoven, that the perplexity cannot be disentangled, nor any reason be assigned why one should be ranged before the other. When the radical idea branches out into parallel ramifications, how can a consecutive series be formed of senses in their nature collateral? The shades of meaning sometimes pass imperceptibly into each other, so that though on one side they apparently differ, yet it is impossible to mark the point of contact. Ideas of the same race, though not exactly alike, are sometimes so little different, that no words can express the dissimilitude, though the mind easily perceives it when they are exhibited together; and sometimes there is such a confusion of acceptations, that discernment is wearied, and distinction puzzled, and perseverance herself hurries to an end, by crowding together what she cannot separate.

These complaints of difficulty will, by those that have never considered words beyond their popular use, be thought only the jargon of a man willing to magnify his labours, and procure veneration to his studies by involution and obscurity. But every art is obscure to those that have not learned it; this uncertainty of terms, and commixture of ideas, is well known to those who have joined philosophy with grammar; and if I have not expressed them very clearly, it must be remembered that I am speaking of that which words are insufficient to explain.

The original sense of words is often driven out of use by their metaphorical acceptations, yet must be inserted for the sake of a regular origination. Thus I know not whether *ardour* is used for *material heat*, or whether *flagrant*, in English, ever signifies the same with *burning*; yet such are the primitive ideas of these words, which are therefore set first, though without examples, that the figurative senses may be commodiously deduced.

Such is the exuberance of signification which many words have obtained, that it was scarcely possible to collect all their senses; sometimes the meaning of derivatives must be sought in the mother term, and sometimes deficient explanations of the primitive may be supplied in the train of derivation. In any case of doubt or difficulty, it will be always proper to examine all the words of the same race; for some words are slightly passed over to avoid repetition, some admitted easier and clearer explanation than others, and all will be better understood, as they are considered in greater variety of structures and relations.

All the interpretations of words are not written with the same skill, or the same happiness: things equally easy in themselves, are not all equally easy to any single mind. Every writer of a long work commits errors, where there appears neither ambiguity to mislead, nor obscurity to confound him; and in a search like this, many felicities of expression will be casually overlooked, many convenient parallels will be forgotten, and many particulars will admit improvement from a mind utterly unequal to the whole performance.

But many seeming faults are to be imputed rather to the nature of the undertaking than the negligence of the performer. Thus some explanations are unavoidably reciprocal or circular, as *hind*, *the female of the stag*; *stag*, *the male of the hind*; sometimes easier words are changed into harder, as, *burial* into *sepulture* or *interment*, *drier* into *desiccative*, *dryness* into *sicity* or *aridity*, *fit* into *paroxysm*; for the easiest word, whatever it be, can never be translated into one more easy. But easiness and difficulty are merely relative; and if the present prevalence of our language should invite foreigners to this Dictionary, many will be assisted by those words which now seem only to increase or produce obscurity. For this reason I have endeavoured frequently to join a Teutonic and Roman interpretation, as to *cheer*, to *gladden*, or *exhilarate*, that every learner of English may be assisted by his own tongue.

The solution of all difficulties, and the supply of all defects, must be sought in the examples, subjoined to the various senses of each word, and ranged according to the time of their authors.

When I first collected these authorities, I was desirous that every quotation should be useful to some other end than the illustration of a word; I therefore extracted from philosophers, principles of science; from historians, remarkable facts; from chemists, complete processes; from divines, striking exhortations; and from poets, beautiful descriptions. Such is design, while it is yet at a distance from execution. When the time called upon me to range this accumulation of elegance and wisdom into an alphabetical series, I soon discovered that the bulk of my volume would fright away the student, and was forced to depart from my scheme of including all that was pleasing or useful in English literature, and reduce my transcripts very often to clusters of words, in which scarcely any meaning is retained; thus to the weariness of copying, I was condemned to add the vexation of expunging. Some passages I have yet spared, which may relieve the labour of verbal searches, and intersperse with verdure and flowers the dusty deserts of barren philology. . . .

Some of the examples have been taken from writers who were never mentioned as masters of elegance, or models of style; but words must be sought where they are used; and in what pages, eminent for purity, can terms of manufacture or agriculture be found? Many quotations serve no other purpose than that of proving the bare existence of words, and are therefore selected with less scrupulousness than those which are to teach their structures and relations.

My purpose was to admit no testimony of living authors, that I might not be misled by partiality, and that none of my contemporaries might have reason to complain; nor have I departed from this resolution, but when some performance of uncommon excellence excited my veneration, when my memory supplied me, from late books, with an example that was wanting, or when my heart, in the tenderness of friendship, solicited admission for a favourite name.

So far have I been from any care to grace my pages with modern decorations, that I have studiously endeavoured to collect examples and authorities from the writers before the Restoration, whose works I regard as "the wells of English undefiled," as the pure sources of genuine diction. Our language, for almost a century, has, by the concurrence of many causes, been gradually departing from its original Teutonic character, and deviating towards a Gallic structure and phraseology, from which it ought to be our endeavour to recal it, by making our ancient volumes the groundwork of style, admitting among the additions of later times, only such as may supply real deficiencies, such as are readily adopted by the genius of our tongue, and incorporate easily with our native idioms.

But as every language has a time of rudeness antecedent to perfection, as well as of false refinement and declension, I have been cautious lest my zeal for antiquity might drive me into times too remote, and crowd my book with words now no longer understood. I have fixed Sidney's work for the boundary, beyond which I make few excursions. From the authors which rose in the time of Elizabeth, a speech might be formed adequate to all purposes of use and elegance. If the language of theology were extracted from Hooker and the translation of the Bible; the terms of natural knowledge from Bacon; the phrases of policy, war, and navigation from Raleigh; the dialect of poetry and fiction from Spenser and Sidney; and the diction of common life from Shakespeare, few ideas would be lost to mankind, for want of English words, in which they might be expressed. . . .

Many terms appropriated to particular occupations, though necessary and significant, are undoubtedly omitted; and of the words most studiously considered and exemplified, many senses have escaped observation.

Yet these failures, however frequent, may admit extenuation and apology. To have attempted much is always laudable, even when the enterprise is above the strength that undertakes it: To rest below his own aim, is incident to every one whose fancy is active, and whose views are comprehensive; nor is any man satisfied with himself because he has done much, but because he can conceive little. When first I engaged in this work, I resolved to leave neither words nor things unexamined, and pleased myself with a prospect of the hours which I should revel away in the feasts of literature, the obscure recesses of northern learning which I should enter and ransack, the treasures with which I expected every search into those neglected mines to reward my labour, and the triumph with which I should display my acquisitions to mankind. When I had thus inquired into the original of words, I resolved to show likewise my attention to things; to pierce deep into every science, to inquire the nature of every substance of which I inserted the name, to limit every idea by a definition strictly logical, and exhibit every production of art or nature in an accurate description, that my book might be in place of all other dictionaries, whether appellative or technical. But these were the dreams of a poet doomed at last to wake a lexicographer. I soon found that it is too late to look for instruments, when the work calls for execution, and that whatever abilities I had brought to my task, with those I must finally perform it. To deliberate whenever I doubted, to inquire whenever I was ignorant, would have protracted the undertaking without end, and, perhaps, without much improvement; for I did not find by my first experiments, that what I had not of my own was easily to be obtained; I saw that one inquiry only gave occasion to another, that book referred to book, that to search was not always to find, and to find was not always to be informed; and that thus to pursue perfection, was, like the first inhabitants of Arcadia, to chase the sun, which, when they had reached the hill where he seemed to rest, was still beheld at the same distance from them.

I then contracted my design, determining to confide in myself, and no longer to solicit auxiliaries, which produced more incumbrances than assistance; by this I obtained at least one advantage, that I set limits to my work, which would in time be ended, though not completed.

Despondency has never so far prevailed as to depress me to negligence; some faults will at last appear to be the effects of anxious diligence and persevering activity. The nice and subtle ramifications of meaning were not easily avoided by a mind intent upon accuracy, and convinced of the necessity of disentangling combinations, and separating similitudes. Many of the distinctions which to common readers appear useless and idle, will be found real and important by men versed in the school of philosophy, without which no dictionary can ever be accurately compiled, or skilfully examined.

Some senses however there are, which, though not the same, are yet so nearly allied, that they are often confounded. Most men think indistinctly, and therefore cannot speak with exactness; and consequently some examples might be indifferently put to either signification: this uncertainty is not to be imputed to me, who do not form, but register the language; who do not teach men how they should think, but relate how they have hitherto expressed their thoughts.

The imperfect sense of some examples I lamented, but could not remedy, and hope they will be compensated by innumerable passages selected with propriety, and preserved with exactness; some shining with sparks of imagination, and some replete with treasures of wisdom. . . .

Of the event of this work, for which, having laboured it with so much application, I cannot have but some degree of parental fondness, it is natural to form conjectures. Those who have been persuaded to think well of my design, will require that it should fix our language, and put a stop to those alterations which time and chance have hitherto been suffered to make in it without opposition. With this consequence I will confess that I flattered myself for awhile; but now begin to fear that I have indulged expectation which neither reason nor experience can justify. When we see men grow old and die at a certain time one after another, from century to century, we laugh at the elixir that promises to prolong life to a thousand years; and with equal justice may the lexicographer be derided, who being able to produce no example of a nation that has preserved their words and phrases from mutability, shall imagine that his dictionary can embalm his language, and secure it from corruption and decay, that it is in his power to change sublunary nature, and clear the world at once from folly, vanity, and affectation.

With this hope, however, academies have been instituted, to guard the avenues of their languages, to retain fugitives, and repulse intruders; but their vigilance and activity have hitherto been vain; sounds are too volatile and subtile for legal restraints; to enchain syllables and to lash the wind, are equally the undertakings of pride, unwilling to measure its desires by its strength. The French language has visibly changed under the inspection of the Academy; the style of Amelot's translation of Father Paul, is observed by Le Courayer to be *un peu passé*; and no Italian will maintain, that the diction of any modern writer is not perceptibly different from that of Boccace, Machiavel, or Caro. . . .

As by the cultivation of various sciences, a language is amplified, it will be more furnished with words deflected from their original sense; the geometrician will talk of a courtier's zenith, or the eccentric virtue of a wild hero, and the physician of sanguine expectations and phlegmatic delays. Copiousness of speech will give opportunities to capricious choice, by which some words will be preferred, and others degraded; vicissitudes of fashion will enforce the use of new, or extend the signification of known terms. The tropes of poetry will make hourly encroachments, and the metaphorical will become the current sense: pronunciation will be varied by levity or ignorance, and the pen must at length comply with the tongue; illiterate writers will, at one time or other, by public infatuation, rise into renown, who not knowing the original import of words, will use them with colloquial licentiousness, confound distinction, and forget propriety. As politeness increases, some expressions will be considered as too gross and vulgar for the delicate, others as too formal and ceremonious for the gay and airy; new phrases are therefore adopted, which must, for the same reasons, be in time dismissed. Swift, in his petty treatise on the English language, allows that new words must sometimes be introduced, but proposes that none should be suffered to become obsolete. But what makes a word obsolete, more than general agreement to forbear it? and how shall it be continued, when it conveys an offensive idea, or recalled again into the mouths of mankind, when it has once become unfamiliar by disuse, and unpleasing by unfamiliarity? . . .

In hope of giving longevity to that which its own nature forbids to be immortal, I have devoted this book, the labour of years, to the honour of my country, that we may no longer yield the palm of philology, without a contest, to the nations of the continent. The chief glory of every people arises from its authors: whether I shall add any thing by my own writings to the reputation of English literature, must be left to time: much of my life has been lost under the pressures of disease; much has been trifled away; and much has always been spent in provision for the day that was passing over me; but I shall not think my employment useless or ignoble, if by my assistance foreign nations and distant ages gain access to the propagators of knowledge, and understand the teachers of truth; if my labours afford light to the repositories of science, and add celebrity to Bacon, to Hooker, to Milton, and to Boyle.

When I am animated by this wish, I look with pleasure on my book, however defective, and deliver it to the world with the spirit of a man that has endeavoured well. That it will immediately become popular, I have not promised to myself: a few wild blunders, and risible absurdities, from which no work of such multiplicity was ever free, may for a time furnish folly with laughter, and harden ignorance into contempt; but useful diligence will at last prevail, and there never can be wanting some who distinguish desert; who will consider that no dictionary of a living tongue ever can be perfect, since, while it is hastening to publication, some words are budding, and some falling away; that a whole life cannot be spent upon syntax and etymology, and that even a whole life would not be sufficient: that he, whose design includes whatever language can express, must often speak of what he does not understand; that a writer will sometimes be hurried by eagerness to the end, and sometimes faint with weariness under a task, which Scaliger compares to the labours of the anvil and the mine; and what is obvious is not always known, and what is known is not always present; that sudden fits of inadvertency will surprise vigilance, slight avocations will seduce attention, and casual eclipses of the mind will darken learning; and that the writer shall often in vain trace his memory at the moment of need, for that which yesterday he knew with intuitive readiness, and which will come uncalled into his thoughts to-morrow.

In this work, when it shall be found that much is omitted, let it not be forgotten that much likewise is performed; and though no book was ever spared out of tenderness to the author, and the world is little solicitous to know whence proceed the faults of that which it condemns; yet it may gratify curiosity to inform it, that the "English Dictionary" was written with little assistance of the learned, and without any patronage of the great; not in the soft obscurities of retirement, or under the shelter of academic bowers, but amidst inconvenience and distraction, in sickness and in sorrow. It may repress the triumph of malignant criticism to observe, that if our language is not here fully displayed, I have only failed in an attempt which no human powers have hitherto completed. If the lexicons of ancient tongues, now immutably fixed, and comprized in a few volumes, be yet, after the toil of successive ages, inadequate and delusive; if the aggregated knowledge and co-operating diligence of

the Italian academicians, did not secure them from the censure of
Beni; if the embodied critics of France, when fifty years had been
spent upon their work, were obliged to change its economy, and give
their second edition another form, I may surely be contented without the praise of perfection, which, if I could obtain, in this gloom
of solitude, what would it avail me? I have protracted my work till
most of those whom I wished to please have sunk into the grave,
and success and miscarriage are empty sounds: I therefore dismiss
it with frigid tranquillity, having little to fear or hope from censure
or from praise.

OLIVER GOLDSMITH
THE VICAR OF WAKEFIELD
1766
Advertisement

THERE are an hundred faults in this thing, and an hundred things might be said to prove them beauties. But it is needless. A book may be amusing with numerous errors, or it may be very dull without a single absurdity. The hero of this piece unites in himself the three greatest characters upon earth; he is a priest, an husbandman, and the father of a family. He is drawn as ready to teach, and ready to obey; as simple in affluence, and majestic in adversity.

In this age of opulence and refinement, whom can such a character please? Such as are fond of high life, will turn with disdain from the simplicity of his country fire-side. Such as mistake ribaldry for humour, will find no wit in his harmless conversation; and such as have been taught to deride religion, will laugh at one, whose chief stores of comfort are drawn from futurity.

OLIVER GOLDSMITH

JAMES BOSWELL

AN ACCOUNT OF CORSICA
Preface to the Third Edition
1769

I NOW beg leave to present the world with a more correct edition of my Account of Corsica. I return my sincere thanks to those who have taken the trouble to point out several faults, with a spirit of candid criticism. I hope they will not be offended that in one or two places I have preserved my own reading, contrary to their opinion; as I never would own that I am wrong, till I am convinced that it is so. My orthography I have sufficiently explained; and although some pleasantry has been shewn, I have not met with one argument against it.

In justice to Mr. Burnaby, I must observe, that the erroneous translation of a passage in Livy, which is corrected in this edition, page 64, was mine; it being no part of his Journal, in which the original text only was quoted. In comparing the former editions with this, it will appear that my first translation renders the meaning of Livy, but does not convey the turn of expression, as I hope I have now done.

While I have a proper sense of my obligations to those who have treated me with candour, I do not forget that there have been others who have chosen to treat me in an illiberal manner. The resentment of some has evidently arisen from the grateful admiration which I have expressed of Mr. Samuel Johnson. Over such, it is a triumph to me, to assure them, that I never cease to think of Mr. Johnson, with the same warmth of affection, and the same dignity of veneration. The resentment of others it is more difficult to explain. For what should make men attack one who never offended them, who has done his best to entertain them, and who is engaged in the most generous cause? But I am told by those who have gone before me in literature, that the attacks of such should rather flatter me, than give me displeasure.

To those who have imagined themselves very witty in sneering at

94

me for being a Christian, I would recommend the serious study of
Theology, and I hope they will attain to the same comfort that I have,
in the belief of a Revelation by which a SAVIOUR is proclaimed
to the world, and "life and immortality are clearly brought to light."

I am now to return thanks to My Lord Lyttelton, for being so
good as to allow me to enrich my book with one of his Lordship's
letters to me. I was indeed most anxious that it should be published;
as it contains an eulogium on Pascal Paoli, equal to any thing that I
have found in the writings of antiquity. Nor can I deny that I was
very desirous to shew the world that this worthy and respectable
Nobleman, to whom genius, learning and virtue owe so much, can
amidst all his literary honours be pleased with what I have been
able to write.

May I be permitted to say that the success of this book has ex-
ceeded my warmest hopes. When I first ventured to send it into
the world, I fairly owned an ardent desire for literary fame.[1] I

[1] In the Preface to the first edition (1768), after some explanations
and acknowledgments Boswell concludes in characteristically personal
style: "He who publishes a book, affecting not to be an authour, and pro-
fessing an indifference for literary fame, may possibly impose upon many
people such an idea of his consequence as he wishes may be received.
For my part I should be proud to be known as an authour; and I have an
ardent ambition for literary fame; for of all possessions I should imagine
literary fame to be the most valuable. A man who has been able to furnish
a book which has been approved by the world, has established himself as a
respectable character in distant society, without any danger of having that
character lessened by the observation of his weaknesses. To preserve an
uniform dignity among those who see us every day, is hardly possible;
and to aim at it, must put us under the fetters of a perpetual restraint.
The authour of an approved book may allow his natural disposition an easy
play, and yet indulge the pride of superiour genius when he considers that
by those who know him only as authour, he never ceases to be respected.
Such an authour when in his hours of gloom and discontent, may have
the consolation to think that his writings are at that very time giving
pleasure to numbers; and such an authour may cherish the hope of being
remembered after death, which has been a great object to the noblest
minds in all ages.

"Whether I may merit any portion of literary fame, the publick will
judge. Whatever my ambition may be, I trust that my confidence is not
too great, nor my hopes too sanguine."

have obtained my desire: and whatever clouds may overcast my days, I can now walk here among the rocks and woods of my ancestors, with an agreeable consciousness that I have done something worthy.

Auchinleck, Ayrshire,
    29 October, 1768

ROBERT BURNS

POEMS

Preface to the Original Edition
Kilmarnock 1786

THE following trifles are not the production of the Poet, who, with all the advantages of learned art, and perhaps amid the elegancies and idlenesses of upper life, looks down for a rural theme, with an eye to Theocrites or Virgil. To the Author of this, these and other celebrated names (their countrymen) are, in their original languages, "a fountain shut up, and a book sealed." Unacquainted with the necessary requisites for commencing Poet by rule, he sings the sentiments and manners he felt and saw in himself and his rustic compeers around him, in his and their native language. Though a Rhymer from his earliest years, at least from the earliest impulses of the softer passions, it was not till very lately that the applause, perhaps the partiality, of Friendship, wakened his vanity so far as to make him think anything of his was worth showing; and none of the following works were ever composed with a view to the press. To amuse himself with the little creations of his own fancy, amid the toil and fatigues of a laborious life; to transcribe the various feelings, the loves, the griefs, the hopes, the fears, in his own breast; to find some kind of counterpoise to the struggles of a world, always an alien scene, a task uncouth to the poetical mind; these were his motives for courting the Muses, and in these he found Poetry to be its own reward.

Now that he appears in the public character of an Author, he does it with fear and trembling. So dear is fame to the rhyming tribe, that even he, an obscure, nameless Bard, shrinks aghast at the thought of being branded as "An impertinent blockhead, obtruding his nonsense on the world; and because he can make a shift to jingle a few doggerel Scotch rhymes together, looks upon himself as a Poet of no small consequence forsooth."

It is an observation of that celebrated Poet—whose divine

Elegies do honour to our language, our nation, and our species[1]—
'that Humility has depressed many a genius to a hermit, but never
raised one to fame.' If any Critic catches at the word *genius*, the
Author tells him, once for all, that he certainly looks upon himself
as possest of some poetic abilities, otherwise his publishing in the
manner he has done, would be a manœuvre below the worst character which, he hopes, his worst enemy will ever give him: but to
the genius of a Ramsay, or the glorious dawnings of the poor, unfortunate Ferguson, he, with equal unaffected sincerity, declares that,
even in his highest pulse of vanity, he has not the most distant pretensions. These two justly admired Scotch Poets he has often had
in his eye in the following pieces; but rather with a view to kindle
at their flame, than for servile imitation.

To his Subscribers the Author returns his most sincere thanks.
Not the mercenary bow over a counter, but the heart-throbbing
gratitude of the Bard, conscious how much he is indebted to Ben-
evolence and Friendship for gratifying him, if he deserves it, in that
dearest wish of every poetic bosom—to be distinguished. He begs
his readers, particularly the Learned and the Polite, who may
honour him with a perusal, that they will make every allowance for
Education and Circumstances of Life: but if, after a fair, candid,
and impartial criticism, he shall stand convicted of Dulness and
Nonsense, let him be done by, as he would in that case do by others
—let him be condemned without mercy, to contempt and oblivion.

[1] William Shenstone: "My favourite authors are of the sentimental
kind—such as Shenstone, particularly in his *Elegies*; Thomson; *Man of
Feeling*—a book I prize next to the Bible; *Man of the Worlds*; Sterne,
especially his *Sentimental Journey*: these are the glorious models after which
I endeavour to form my conduct, etc. etc." *Burns to John Murdoch*,
15th January 1783.

WILLIAM BLAKE

MILTON

A POEM IN TWO BOOKS
TO JUSTIFY THE WAYS OF GOD TO MEN

1804

Preface

THE Stolen and Perverted Writings of Homer and Ovid, of Plato and Cicero, which all Men ought to contemn, are set up by artifice against the Sublime of the Bible; but when the New Age is at leisure to Pronounce, all will be set right, and those Grand Works of the more ancient and consciously and professedly Inspired Men will hold their proper rank, and the Daughters of Memory shall become the Daughters of Inspiration. Shakespeare and Milton were both curb'd by the general malady and infection from the silly Greek and Latin slaves of the Sword. Rouze up, O Young Men of the New Age! Set your foreheads against the ignorant Hirelings! For we have Hirelings in the Camp, the Court and the University, who would, if they could, for ever depress Mental and prolong Corporeal War. Painters! on you I call. Sculptors! Architects! Suffer not the fashionable Fools to depress your powers by the prices they pretend to give for contemptible works, or the expensive advertizing boasts that they make of such works: believe Christ and his Apostles that there is a Class of Men whose whole delight is in Destroying. We do not want either Greek or Roman Models if we are but just and true to our own Imaginations, those Worlds of Eternity in which we shall live for ever in JESUS OUR LORD.

> *And did those feet in ancient time*
> *Walk upon England's mountains green?*
> *And was the holy Lamb of God*
> *On England's pleasant pastures seen?*
>
> *And did the Countenance Divine*
> *Shine forth upon our clouded hills?*
> *And was Jerusalem builded here*
> *Among these dark Satanic Mills?*

99

Bring me my Bow of burning gold:
Bring me my Arrows of desire:
Bring me my Spear: O clouds unfold!
Bring me my Chariot of fire.

I will not cease from Mental Fight,
Nor shall my Sword sleep in my hand
Till we have built Jerusalem
In England's green and pleasant Land.

"Would to God that all the Lord's people were Prophets."—
NUMBERS, xi. ch., 29 v.

WILLIAM WORDSWORTH

LYRICAL BALLADS

Preface to Editions of 1800–1802

. . . THE principal object, then, proposed in these Poems was to choose incidents and situations from common life, and to relate or describe them, throughout, as far as was possible in a selection of language really used by men, and, at the same time, to throw over them a certain colouring of imagination, whereby ordinary things should be presented to the mind in an unusual aspect; and, further, and above all, to make these incidents and situations interesting by tracing in them, truly though not ostentatiously, the primary laws of our nature: chiefly, as far as regards the manner in which we associate ideas in a state of excitement. Humble and rustic life was generally chosen, because, in that condition, the essential passions of the heart find a better soil in which they can attain their maturity, are less under restraint, and speak a plainer and more emphatic language; because in that condition of life our elementary feelings co-exist in a state of greater simplicity, and, consequently, may be more accurately contemplated, and more forcibly com-municated; because the manners of rural life germinate from those elementary feelings, and, from the necessary character of rural occu-pations, are more easily comprehended, and are more durable; and, lastly, because in that condition the passions of men are incorporated with the beautiful and permanent forms of Nature. The language, too, of these men has been adopted (purified indeed from what appear to be its real defects, from all lasting and rational causes of dislike or disgust) because such men hourly communicate with the best objects from which the best part of language is originally derived; and because, from their rank in society and the sameness and narrow circle of their intercourse, being less under the influence of social vanity, they convey their feelings and notions in simple and unelaborated expressions. Accordingly, such a language, arising out of repeated experience and regular feelings, is a more permanent, and a far more philosophical language, than that which is frequently substituted for it by Poets, who think that they are conferring honour upon themselves and their art, in proportion as they separate themselves from the sympathies of men, and indulge in arbitrary and capricious habits of expression, in order to furnish food for fickle tastes, and fickle appetites, of their own creation.

I cannot, however, be insensible to the present outcry against the triviality and meanness, both of thought and language, which some of my contemporaries have occasionally introduced into their metrical compositions; and I acknowledge that this defect, where it exists, is more dishonourable to the Writer's own character than false refinement or arbitrary innovation, though I should contend at the same time, that it is far less pernicious in the sum of its consequences. From such verses the Poems in these volumes will be found distinguished at least by one mark of difference, that each of them has a worthy *purpose*. Not that I always began to write with a distinct purpose formally conceived; but habits of meditation have, I trust, so prompted and regulated my feelings, that my descriptions of such objects as strongly excite those feelings, will be found to carry along with them a *purpose*. If this opinion be erroneous, I can have little right to the name of a Poet. For all good poetry is the spontaneous overflow of powerful feelings: and though this be true, Poems to which any value can be attached were never produced on any variety of subjects but by a man who, being possessed of more than usual organic sensibility, had also thought long and deeply. For our continued influxes of feeling are modified and directed by our thoughts, which are indeed the representatives of all our past feelings; and, as by contemplating the relation of these general representatives to each other, we discover what is really important to men, so, by the repetition and continuance of this act, our feelings will be connected with important subjects, till at length, if we be originally possessed of much sensibility, such habits of mind will be produced, that, by obeying blindly and mechanically the impulses of those habits, we shall describe objects, and utter sentiments, of such a nature, and in such connection with each other, that the understanding of the Reader must necessarily be in some degree enlightened, and his affections strengthened and purified.

It has been said that each of these poems has a purpose. Another circumstance must be mentioned which distinguishes these Poems from the popular Poetry of the day; it is this, that the feeling therein developed gives importance to the action and situation, and not the action and situation to the feeling.

A sense of false modesty shall not prevent me from asserting, that the Reader's attention is pointed to this mark of distinction, far less for the sake of these particular Poems than from the general importance of the subject. The subject is indeed important! For the human mind is capable of being excited without the application of gross and violent stimulants; and he must have a very faint perception of its beauty and dignity who does not know this, and who does not further know, that one being is elevated above another, in proportion as he possesses this capability. It has therefore appeared to me, that to endeavour to produce or enlarge this capability is one of the best services in which, at any period, a Writer can be engaged; but this service, excellent at all times, is especially so at the present day. For a multitude of causes, unknown to former times, are now acting with a combined force to blunt the discriminating powers of the mind, and, unfitting it for all voluntary exertion, to reduce it to a state of almost savage torpor. The most effective of these causes are the great national events which are daily taking place, and the increasing accumulation of men in cities, where the uniformity of their occupations produces a craving for extraordinary incident, which the rapid communication of intelligence hourly gratifies. To this tendency of life and manners the literature and theatrical exhibitions of the country have conformed themselves. The invaluable works of our elder writers, I had almost said the works of Shakespeare and Milton, are driven into neglect by frantic novels, sickly and stupid German Tragedies, and deluges of idle and extravagant stories in verse.—When I think upon this degrading thirst after outrageous stimulation, I am almost ashamed to have spoken of the feeble endeavour made in these volumes to counteract it; and, reflecting upon the magnitude of the general evil, I should be oppressed with no dishonourable melancholy, had I not a deep impression of certain inherent and indestructible qualities of the human mind, and likewise of certain powers in the great and permanent objects that act upon it, which are equally inherent and indestructible; and were there not added to this impression a belief, that the time is approaching when the evil will be systematically opposed, by men of greater powers, and with far more distinguished success. . . .

Taking up the subject, then, upon general grounds, let me ask, what is meant by the word Poet? What is a Poet? To whom does he address himself? And what language is to be expected from him?—He is a man speaking to men: a man, it is true, endowed with more lively sensibility, more enthusiasm and tenderness, who has a greater knowledge of human nature, and a more comprehensive soul, than are supposed to be common among mankind; a man pleased with his own passions and volitions, and who rejoices more than other men in the spirit of life that is in him; delighting to contemplate similar volitions and passions as manifested in the goings-on of the Universe, and habitually impelled to create them where he does not find them. To these qualities he has added a disposition to be affected more than other men by absent things as if they were present; an ability of conjuring up in himself passions, which are indeed far from being the same as those produced by real events, yet (especially in those parts of the general sympathy which are pleasing and delightful) do more nearly resemble the passions produced by real events, than anything which, from the motions of their own minds merely, other men are accustomed to feel in themselves:—whence, and from practice, he has acquired a greater readiness and power in expressing what he thinks and feels, and especially those thoughts and feelings which, by his own choice, or from the structure of his own mind, arise in him without immediate external excitement.

But whatever portion of this faculty we may suppose even the greatest Poet to possess, there cannot be a doubt that the language which it will suggest to him, must often, in liveliness and truth, fall short of that which is uttered by men in real life, under the actual pressure of those passions, certain shadows of which the Poet thus produces, or feels to be produced, in himself. . . .

The Poet writes under one restriction only, namely, the necessity of giving immediate pleasure to a human Being possessed of that information which may be expected from him, not as a lawyer, a physician, a mariner, an astronomer, or a natural philosopher, but as a Man. Except this one restriction, there is no object standing between the Poet and the image of things; between this, and the Biographer and Historian, there are a thousand.

Nor let this necessity of producing immediate pleasure be considered as a degradation of the Poet's art. It is far otherwise. It is an acknowledgement of the beauty of the universe, an acknowledgement the more sincere, because not formal, but indirect; it is a task light and easy to him who looks at the world in the spirit of love: further, it is a homage paid to the native and naked dignity of man, to the grand elementary principle of pleasure, by which he knows, and feels, and lives, and moves. We have no sympathy but what is propagated by pleasure: I would not be misunderstood; but wherever we sympathise with pain, it will be found that the sympathy is produced and carried on by subtle combinations with pleasure. We have no knowledge, that is, no general principles drawn from the contemplation of particular facts, but what has been built up by pleasure, and exists in us by pleasure alone. The Man of science, the Chemist and Mathematician, whatever difficulties and disgusts they may have had to struggle with, know and feel this. However painful may be the objects with which the Anatomist's knowledge is connected, he feels that his knowledge is pleasure; and where he has no pleasure he has no knowledge. What then does the Poet? He considers man and the objects that surround him as acting and re-acting upon each other, so as to produce an infinite complexity of pain and pleasure; he considers man in his own nature and in his ordinary life as contemplating this with a certain quantity of immediate knowledge, with certain convictions, intuitions, and deductions, which from habit acquire the quality of intuitions; he considers him as looking upon this complex scene of ideas and sensations, and finding every where objects that immediately excite in him sympathies which, from the necessities of his nature, are accompanied by an overbalance of enjoyment.

To this knowledge which all men carry about with them, and to these sympathies in which, without any other discipline than that of our daily life, we are fitted to take delight, the Poet principally directs his attention. He considers man and nature as essentially adapted to each other, and the mind of man as naturally the mirror of the fairest and most interesting properties of nature. And thus the Poet, prompted by this feeling of pleasure, which accompanies him through the whole course of his studies, converses with general nature, with affections akin to those, which, through labour and length of time, the Man of science has raised up in himself, by conversing with those particular parts of nature which are the objects of his studies. The knowledge both of the Poet and the Man of science is pleasure; but the knowledge of the one cleaves to us as a necessary part of our existence, our natural and unalienable inheritance; the other is a personal and individual acquisition, slow to come to us, and by no habitual and direct sympathy connecting us with our fellow-beings. The Man of science seeks truth as a remote and unknown benefactor; he cherishes and loves it in his solitude: the Poet, singing a song in which all human beings join with him, rejoices in the presence of truth as our visible friend and hourly companion. Poetry is the breath and finer spirit of all knowledge; it is the impassioned expression which is in the countenance of all Science. Emphatically may it be said of the Poet, as Shakespeare hath said of man, "that he looks before and after." He is the rock of defence for human nature; an upholder and preserver, carrying every where with him relationship and love. In spite of difference of soil and climate, of language and manners, of laws and customs: in spite of things silently gone out of mind, and things violently destroyed; the Poet binds together by passion and knowledge the vast empire of human society, as it is spread over the whole earth, and over all time. The objects of the Poet's thoughts are every where; though the eyes and senses of man are, it is true, his favourite guides, yet he will follow wheresoever he can find an atmosphere of sensation in which to move his wings. Poetry is the first and last of all knowledge—it is as immortal as the heart of man. If the labours of Men of science should ever create any material revolution, direct or indirect, in our condition, and in the impressions which we habitually receive, the Poet will sleep then no more than at present; he will be ready to follow the steps of the Man of science, not only in those general indirect effects, but he will be at his side, carrying sensation into the midst of the objects of the science itself. The remotest discoveries of the Chemist, the Botanist, or Mineralogist, will be as proper objects of the Poet's art as any upon which it can be employed, if the time should ever come when these things shall be familiar to us, and the relations under which they are contemplated by the followers of these respective sciences shall be manifestly and palpably material to us as enjoying and suffering beings. If the time should ever come when what is now called science, thus familiarised to men, shall be ready to put on, as it were, a form of flesh and blood, the Poet will lend his divine spirit to aid the transfiguration, and will welcome the Being thus produced, as a dear and genuine inmate of the household of man.— It is not, then, to be supposed that any one, who holds that sublime notion of Poetry which I have attempted to convey, will break in upon the sanctity and truth of his pictures by transitory and accidental ornaments, and endeavour to excite admiration of himself by arts, the necessity of which must manifestly depend upon the assumed meanness of his subject. . . .

WILLIAM WORDSWORTH

Letter to the Right. Hon.
CHARLES JAMES FOX

Grasmere, Westmoreland, January 14th, 1801

SIR,

It is not without much difficulty, that I have summoned the courage to request your acceptance of these Volumes. Should I express my real feelings, I am sure that I should seem to make a parade of diffidence and humility.

Several of the poems contained in these Volumes are written upon subjects, which are the common property of all Poets, and which, at some period of your life, must have been interesting to a man of your sensibility, and perhaps may still continue to be so. It would be highly gratifying to me to suppose that even in a single instance the manner in which I have treated these general topics should afford you any pleasure; but such a hope does not influence me upon the present occasion; in truth I do not feel it. Besides, I am convinced that there must be many things in this collection, which may impress you with an unfavourable idea of my intellectual powers. I do not say this with a wish to degrade myself; but I am sensible that this must be the case, from the different circles in which we have moved, and the different objects with which we have been conversant.

Being utterly unknown to you as I am, I am well aware, that if I am justified in writing to you at all, it is necessary, my letter should be short; but I have feelings within me which I hope will so far shew themselves in this Letter as to excuse the trespass which I am afraid I shall make. In common with the whole of the English People I have observed in your public character a constant predominance of sensibility of heart. Necessitated as you have been from your public situation to have much to do with men in bodies, and in classes, and accordingly to contemplate them in that relation, it has been your praise that you have not thereby been prevented from looking upon them as individuals, and that you have habitually left your heart open to be influenced by them in that capacity. This habit cannot but have made you dear to Poets; and I am sure that, if since your first entrance into public life there has been a single true poet living in England, he must have loved you.

But were I assured that I myself had a just claim to the title of a Poet, all the dignity being attached to the Word which belongs to it, I do not think that I should have ventured for that reason to offer these volumes to you: at present it is solely on account of two poems in the second volume, the one entitled "*The Brothers*," and the other "*Michael*," that I have been emboldened to take this liberty.

It appears to me that the most calamitous effect, which has followed the measures which have lately been pursued in this country, is a rapid decay of the domestic affections among the lower orders of society. This effect the present Rulers of this Country are not conscious of, or they disregard it. For many years past, the tendency of society amongst almost all the nations of Europe has been to produce it. But recently by the spreading of manufactures through every part of the country, by the heavy taxes upon postage, by workhouses, Houses of Industry, and the invention of Soup-shops &c. &c. superadded to the encreasing disproportion between the price of labour and that of the necessaries of life, the bonds of domestic feeling among the poor, as far as the influence of these things has extended, have been weakened, and in innumerable instances entirely destroyed. The evil would be the less to be regretted, if these institutions were regarded only as palliatives to a disease; but the vanity and pride of their promoters are so subtly interwoven with them, that they are deemed great discoveries and blessings to humanity. In the mean time parents are separated from their children, and children from their parents; the wife no longer prepares with her own hands a meal for her husband, the produce of his labour; there is little doing in his house in which his affections can be interested, and but little left in it which he can love. I have two neighbours, a man and his wife, both upwards of eighty years of age; they live alone; the husband has been confined to his bed many months and has never had, nor till within these few weeks has ever needed, any body to attend to him but his wife. She has recently been seized with a lameness which has often prevented her from being able to carry him his food to his bed; the neighbours fetch water for her from the well, and do other kind offices for them both, but her infirmities encrease. She told my Servant two days ago that she was afraid they must both be boarded out among some other Poor of the parish (they have long been supported by the parish) but she said, it was hard, having kept house together so long, to come to this, and she was sure that "it would burst her heart." I mention this fact to shew how deeply the spirit of independence is, even yet, rooted in some parts of the country. These people could not express themselves in this way without an almost sublime conviction of the blessings of independent domestic life. If it is true, as I believe, that this spirit is rapidly disappearing, no greater curse can befal a land.

I earnestly entreat your pardon for having detained you so long. In the two poems, "The Brothers" and "Michael," I have attempted to draw a picture of the domestic affections as I know they exist amongst a class of men who are now almost confined to the North of England. They are small independent *proprietors* of land here called statesmen, men of respectable education who daily labour on their own little properties. The domestic affections will always be strong amongst men who live in a country not crowded with population, if these men are placed above poverty. But if they are pro-prietors of small estates, which have descended to them from their ancestors, the power which these affections will acquire amongst such men is inconceivable by those who have only had an oppor-tunity of observing hired labourers, farmers, and the manufacturing Poor. Their little tract of land serves as a kind of permanent rallying point for their domestic feelings, as a tablet upon which they are written, which makes them objects of memory in a thousand instances when they would otherwise be forgotten. It is a fountain fitted to the nature of social man from which supplies of affection, as pure as his heart was intended for, are daily drawn. This class of men is rapidly disappearing. You, Sir, have a consciousness, upon which every good man will congratulate you, that the whole of your public conduct has in one way or other been directed to the pre-servation of this class of men, and those who hold similar situations.

You have felt that the most sacred of all property is the property of the Poor. The two Poems which I have mentioned were written with a view to shew that men who do not wear fine cloaths can feel deeply. "Pectus enim est quod disertos facit, et vis mentis. Ideoque imperitis quoque, si modo sint aliquo affectu concitati, verba non desunt." The poems are faithful copies from nature; and I hope, whatever effect they may have upon you, you will at least be able to perceive that they may excite profitable sympathies in many kind and good hearts, and may in some small degree enlarge our feelings of reverence for our species, and our knowledge of human nature, by shewing that our best qualities are possessed by men whom we are too apt to consider, not with reference to the points in which they resemble us, but to those in which they manifestly differ from us. I thought, at a time when these feelings are sapped in so many ways, that the two poems might co-operate, however feebly, with the illustrious efforts which you have made to stem this and other evils with which the country is labouring, and it is on this account alone that I have taken the liberty of thus addressing you.

Wishing earnestly that the time may come when the country may perceive what it has lost by neglecting your advice, and hoping that your latter days may be attended with health and comfort.

I remain, With the highest respect and admiration,
Your most obedient and humble Servt

W. WORDSWORTH

Address: The Right Honble Charles James Fox.

LORD BYRON

HOURS OF IDLENESS
1807
Preface

IN submitting to the public eye the following collection, I have not only to combat the difficulties that writers of verse generally encounter, but may incur the charge of presumption for obtruding myself on the world, when, without doubt, I might be, at my age, more usefully employed.

These productions are the fruits of the lighter hours of a young man who has lately completed his nineteenth year. As they bear the internal evidence of a boyish mind, this is, perhaps, unnecessary information. Some few were written during the disadvantages of illness and depression of spirits: under the former influence CHILDISH RECOLLECTIONS, in particular, were composed. This consideration, though it cannot excite the voice of praise, may at least arrest the arm of censure. A considerable portion of these poems has been privately printed, at the request and for the perusal of my friends. I am sensible that the partial and frequently injudicious admiration of a social circle is not the criterion by which poetical genius is to be estimated, yet "to do greatly," we must "dare greatly"; and I have hazarded my reputation and feelings in publishing this volume. I have "passed the Rubicon" and must stand or fall by the "cast of the die." In the latter event, I shall submit without a murmur; for, though *not* without solicitude for the fate of these effusions, my expectations are by no means sanguine. It is probable that I may have dared much and done little; for, in the words of Cowper, "it is one thing to write what may please our friends, who, because they are such, are apt to be a little biassed in our favour, and another to write what may please everybody; because they who have no connection, or even knowledge of the author, will be sure to find fault if they can." To the truth of this, however, I do not wholly subscribe; on the contrary, I feel convinced that these trifles will not be treated with injustice. Their merit, if they possess any, will be liberally allowed; their numerous faults, on the other hand, cannot expect that favour which has been denied to others of maturer years, decided character, and far greater ability.

I have not aimed at exclusive originality, still less have I studied any particular model for imitation; some translations are given, of which many are paraphrastic. In the original pieces there may appear a casual coincidence with authors whose works I have been accustomed to read; but I have not been guilty of intentional plagiarism. To produce anything entirely new, in an age so fertile in rhyme, would be a Herculean task, as every subject has already been treated to its utmost extent. Poetry, however, is not my primary vocation; to divert the dull moments of indisposition, or the monotony of a vacant hour, urged me "to this sin": little can be expected from so unpromising a muse. My wreath, scanty as it must be, is all I shall derive from these productions; and I shall never attempt to replace its fading leaves, or pluck a single additional sprig from groves where I am, at best, an intruder. Though accustomed, in my younger days, to rove a careless mountaineer on the Highlands of Scotland, I have not, of late years, had the benefit of such pure air, or so elevated a residence, as might enable me to enter the lists with genuine bards who have enjoyed both these advantages. But they derive considerable fame, and a few not less profit, from their productions; while I shall expiate my rashness as an interloper, certainly without the latter, and in all probability with a very slight share of the former. I leave to others "virum volitare per ora." I look to the few who will hear with patience, "dulce est desipere in loco." To the former worthies I resign, without repining, the hope of immortality, and content myself with the not very magnificent prospect of ranking amongst "the mob of gentlemen who write";—my readers must determine whether I dare say "with ease," or the honour of a posthumous page in "The Catalogue of Royal and Noble Authors,"—a work to which the Peerage is under infinite obligations, inasmuch as many names of considerable length, sound, and antiquity, are thereby rescued from the obscurity which unluckily overshadows several voluminous productions of their illustrious bearers.

With slight hopes, and some fears, I publish this first and last attempt. To the dictates of young ambition may be ascribed many actions more criminal and equally absurd. To a few of my own age the contents may afford amusement; I trust they will, at least, be found harmless. It is highly improbable, for my situation and pursuits hereafter, that I should ever obtrude myself a second time on the public; nor even, in the very doubtful event of present indulgence, shall I be tempted to commit a future trespass of the same nature. The opinion of Dr. Johnson on the poems of a noble relation[1] of mine, "That when a man of rank appeared in the character of an author, he deserved to have his merit handsomely allowed," can have little weight with verbal, and still less with periodical, censors; but were it otherwise, I should be loth to avail myself of the privilege, and would rather incur the bitterest censure of anonymous criticism, than triumph in honours granted solely to a title.

[1] "The Earl of Carlisle, whose works have long received the meed of public applause, to which, by their intrinsic worth, they were well entitled."

In *English Bards and Scotch Reviewers*, with which Byron replied to the contemptuous review in *The Edinburgh Review* of these poems, Byron is not so courteous to his noble relative:

> "Let Stott, Carlisle, Matilda and the rest
> Of Grub Street and of Grosvenor Place the best,
> Scrawl on, 'till death release us from the strain,
> Or common-sense assert her rights again."

LORD BYRON

DON JUAN

1819

Dedication

I

Bob Southey! You're a poet—Poet-laureate,
  And representative of all the race;
Although 'tis true that you turned out a Tory at
  Last,—yours has lately been a common case;
And now, my Epic Renegade! what are ye at?
  With all the Lakers, in and out of place?
A nest of tuneful persons, to my eye
Like "four and twenty Blackbirds in a pye;

II

"Which pye being open'd they began to sing,"
  (This old song and new simile holds good),
"A dainty dish to set before the King,"
  Or Regent, who admires such kind of food;—
And Coleridge, too, has lately taken wing,
  But like a hawk encumbered with his hood,—
Explaining Metaphysics to the nation—
I wish he would explain his Explanation.

III

You, Bob! are rather insolent, you know,
  At being disappointed in your wish
To supersede all warblers here below,
  And be the only Blackbird in the dish;
And then you overstrain yourself, or so,
  And tumble downward like the flying fish
Gasping on deck, because you soar too high, Bob,
And fall, for lack of moisture, quite a-dry, Bob!

115

IV

And Wordsworth, in a rather long "Excursion"
  (I think the quarto holds five hundred pages),
Has given a sample from the vasty version
  Of his new system to perplex the sages;
'Tis poetry—at least by his assertion,
  And may appear so when the dog-star rages—
And he who understands it would be able
To add a story to the Tower of Babel.

V

You—Gentlemen! by dint of long seclusion
  From better company, have kept your own
At Keswick, and, through still continued fusion
  Of one another's minds, at last have grown
To deem, as a most logical conclusion,
  That Poesy has wreaths for you alone:
There is a narrowness in such a notion,
Which makes me wish you'd change your lakes for Ocean.

VI

I would not imitate the petty thought,
  Nor coin my self-love to so base a vice,
For all the glory your conversion brought,
  Since gold alone should not have been its price.
You have your salary; was't for that you wrought?
  And Wordsworth has his place in the Excise.
You're shabby fellows—true—but poets still,
And duly seated on the Immortal Hill.

VII

Your bays may hide the baldness of your brows—
  Perhaps some virtuous blushes;—let them go—
To you I envy neither fruit nor boughs—
  And for the fame you would engross below,
The field is universal, and allows
  Scope to all such as feel the inherent glow:

Scott, Rogers, Campbell, Moore, and Crabbe, will try
'Gainst you the question with posterity.

VIII

For me, who, wandering with pedestrian Muses,
   Contend not with you on the wingéd steed,
I wish your fate may yield ye, when she chooses,
   The fame you envy, and the skill you need;
And, recollect, a poet nothing loses
   In giving to his brethren their full meed
Of merit—and complaint of present days
Is not the certain path to future praise.

IX

He that reserves his laurels for posterity
   (Who does not often claim the bright reversion)
Has generally no great crop to spare it, he
   Being only injured by his own assertion;
And although here and there some glorious rarity
   Arise like Titan from the sea's immersion,
The major part of such appellants go
To—God knows where—for no one else can know.

X

If, fallen in evil days on evil tongues,
   Milton appealed to the Avenger, Time,
If Time, the Avenger, execrates his wrongs,
   And makes the word "Miltonic" mean "*Sublime*,"
He deigned not to belie his soul in songs,
   Nor turn his very talent to a crime;
He did not loathe the Sire to laud the Son,
But closed the tyrant-hater he began.

XI

Think'st thou, could he—the blind Old Man—arise
   Like Samuel from the grave, to freeze once more
The blood of monarchs with his prophecies,
   Or be alive again—again all hoar

With time and trials, and those helpless eyes,
   And heartless daughters—worn—and pale—and poor;
Would *he* adore a sultan? *he* obey
The intellectual eunuch Castlereagh? . . .

XV

If we may judge of matter by the mind,
   Emasculated to the marrow *It*
Hath but two objects, how to serve, and bind,
   Deeming the chain it wears even men may fit,
Entropius of its many masters,—blind
   To worth as freedom, wisdom as to wit,
Fearless—because *no* feeling dwells in ice,
Its very courage stagnates to a vice.

XVI

Where shall I turn me not to *view* its bonds,
   For I will never *feel* them?—Italy!
Thy late reviving Roman soul desponds
   Beneath the lie this State-thing breathed o'er thee—
Thy clanking chain, and Erin's yet green wounds,
   Have voices—tongues to cry aloud for me.
Europe has slaves—allies—kings—armies still—
And Southey lives to sing them very ill.

XVII

Meantime, Sir Laureate, I proceed to dedicate,
   In honest simple verse, this song to you.
And, if in flattering strains I do not predicate,
   'Tis that I still retain my "buff and blue";
My politics as yet are all to educate:
   Apostasy's so fashionable, too,
To keep *one* creed's a task grown quite Herculean;
Is it not so, my Tory, ultra-Julian?

                 Venice, Sept. 16, 1818.

JOHN KEATS

ENDYMION

A POETIC ROMANCE

1818

Inscribed to the Memory of Thomas Chatterton

Preface

KNOWING within myself the manner in which this Poem has been produced it is not without a feeling of regret that I make it public.

What manner I mean, will be quite clear to the reader, who must soon perceive great inexperience, immaturity, and every error denoting a feverish attempt, rather than a deed accomplished. The two first books, and indeed the two last, I feel sensible are not of such completion as to warrant their passing the press; nor should they if I thought a year's castigation would do them any good;—it will not: the foundations are too sandy. It is just that this youngster should die away: a sad thought for me, if I had not some hope that while it is dwindling I may be plotting, and fitting myself for verses fit to live.

This may be speaking too presumptuously, and may deserve a punishment; but no feeling man will be forward to inflict it: he will leave me alone, with the conviction that there is not a fiercer hell than the failure in a great object. This is not written with the least atom of purpose to forestall criticisms of course, but from the desire I have to conciliate men who are competent to look, and who do look with a zealous eye, to the honour of English literature. The imagination of a boy is healthy, and the mature imagination of a man is healthy; but there is a space of life between, in which the soul is in a ferment, the character undecided, the way of life uncertain, the ambition thick-sighted thence proceed: mawkishness, and all the thousand bitters which those men I speak of must necessarily taste in going over the following pages.

I hope I have not in too late a day touched the beautiful mythology of Greece, and dulled its brightness: for I wish to try once more, before I bid it farewel.

Teignmouth,
April 10, 1818.

CHARLES LAMB

WORKS

1818

Dedication to S. T. Coleridge, Esq.

MY DEAR COLERIDGE—You will smile to see the slender labours of your friend designated by the title of *Works*; but such was the wish of the gentlemen who have kindly undertaken the trouble of collecting them, and from their judgment could be no appeal.

It would be a kind of disloyalty to offer to any one but yourself a volume containing the *early pieces*, which were first published among your poems, and were fairly derivatives from you and them. My friend Lloyd and myself came into our first battle (authorship is a sort of warfare) under cover of the greater Ajax. How this association, which shall always be a dear and proud recollection to me, came to be broken,—who snapped the threefold cord,—whether yourself (but I know that was not the case) grew ashamed of your former companions,—or whether (which is by much the more probable) some ungracious bookseller was author of the separation,—I cannot tell;—but wanting the support of your friendly elm, (I speak for myself), my vine has, since that time, put forth few or no fruits; the sap (if ever it had any) has become, in a manner, dried up and extinct; and you will find your old associate, in his second volume, dwindled into prose and *criticism*.

Am I right in assuming this as the cause? or is it that, as years come upon us, (except with some more healthy-happy spirits,) Life itself loses much of its Poetry for us? we transcribe but what we read in the great volume of Nature; and, as the characters grow dim, we turn off, and look another way. You yourself write no more Christabels, nor Ancient Mariners, now.

Some of the Sonnets, which shall be carefully turned over by the general reader, may happily awaken in your remembrances, which I should be sorry should be ever totally extinct—the memory

Of summer days and of delightful years—

even so far back as to those old suppers at our old ———[1] Inn,— when life was fresh, and topics exhaustless,—and you first kindled in me, if not the power, yet the love of poetry, and beauty, and kindliness.—

> *What words have I heard*
> *Spoke at the Mermaid!*

The world has given you many a shrewd nip and gird since that time, but either my eyes are grown dimmer, or my old friend is the *same*, who stood before me three-and-twenty years ago—his hair a little confessing the hand of Time, but still shrouding the same capacious brain,—his heart not altered, scarcely where it "alteration finds."

One piece, Coleridge, I have ventured to publish in its original form, though I have heard you complain of a certain over-imitation of the antique in the style. If I could see any way of getting rid of the objection, without re-writing it entirely, I would make some sacrifices. But when I wrote John Woodvil, I never proposed to myself any distinct deviation from common English. I had been newly initiated in the writings of our elder dramatists: Beaumont and Fletcher, and Massinger were then a *first love*; and from what I was so freshly conversant in, what wonder if my language imperceptibly took a tinge? The very *time*, which I had chosen for my story, that which immediately followed the Restoration, seemed to require, in an English play, that the English should be of rather an older cast than that of the precise year in which it happened to be written. I wish it had not some faults, which I can less vindicate than the language. I remain, My dear Coleridge, Yours, with unabated esteem.

C. Lamb.

[1] Salutation.

PERCY BYSSHE SHELLEY

PROMETHEUS UNBOUND
A LYRICAL DRAMA
1820

Audisne haec Amphiarae, sub terram abdite?

Preface

THE Greek tragic writers, in selecting as their subject any portion of their national history or mythology, employed in their treatment of it a certain arbitrary discretion. They by no means conceived themselves bound to adhere to the common interpretation, or to imitate in story, as in title, their rivals and predecessors. Such a system would have amounted to a resignation of those claims to preference over their competitors which incited the composition. The Agamemnonian story was exhibited on the Athenian theatre with as many variations as dramas.

I have presumed to employ a similar license. The *Prometheus Unbound* of Aeschylus supposed the reconciliation of Jupiter with his victim as the price of the disclosure of the danger threatened to his empire by the consummation of his marriage with Thetis. Thetis, according to this view of the subject, was given in marriage to Peleus, and Prometheus, by the permission of Jupiter, delivered from his captivity by Hercules. Had I framed my story on this model, I should have done no more than have attempted to restore the lost drama of Aeschylus; an ambition, which, if my preference to this mode of treating the subject had incited me to cherish, the recollection of the high comparison such an attempt would challenge might well abate. But, in truth, I was averse from a catastrophe so feeble as that of reconciling the Champion with the Oppressor of mankind. The moral interest of the fable, which is so powerfully sustained by the sufferings and endurance of Prometheus, would be annihilated if we could conceive of him as unsaying his high language and quailing before his successful and perfidious adversary. The only imaginary being resembling in any degree Prometheus, is Satan: and Prometheus is, in my judgement, a more poetical character than Satan, because, in addition to courage and majesty, and firm and patient opposition to omnipotent force, he is susceptible of being described as exempt from the taints of ambition, envy, revenge, and a desire for personal aggrandisement, which, in the Hero of *Paradise Lost*, interfere with the interest. The character of Satan engenders in the mind a pernicious casuistry which leads us to weigh his faults with his wrongs, and to excuse the former because the latter exceed all measure. In the minds of those who consider that magnificent fiction with a religious feeling, it engenders something worse. But Prometheus is, as it were, the type of the highest perfection of moral and intellectual nature, impelled by the purest and the truest motives to the best and noblest ends.

This Poem was chiefly written upon the mountainous ruins of the Baths of Caracalla, among the flowery glades, and thickets of odoriferous blossoming trees, which are extended in ever-winding labyrinths upon its immense platforms and dizzy arches suspended in the air. The bright blue sky of Rome, and the effect of the vigorous awakening of spring in that divinest climate, and the new life with which it drenches the spirits even to intoxication, were the inspiration of this drama.

The imagery which I have employed will be found, in many instances, to have been drawn from the operations of the human mind, or from those external actions by which they are expressed. This is unusual in modern poetry, although Dante and Shakespeare are full of instances of the same kind: Dante indeed more than any other poet, and with greater success. But the Greek poets, as writers to whom no resource of awakening the sympathy of their contemporaries was unknown, were in the habitual use of this power; and it is the study of their works (since a higher merit would probably be denied me), to which I am willing that my readers should impute this singularity.

One word is due in candour to the degree in which the study of contemporary writings may have tinged my composition, for such has been a topic of censure with regard to poems far more popular, and, indeed, deservedly popular, than mine. It is impossible that any one who inhabits the same age with such writers as those who stand in the foremost ranks of our own, can conscientiously assure himself that his language and tone of thought may not have been modified by the study of the productions of those extraordinary intellects. It is true, that, not the spirit of their genius, but the forms in which it has manifested itself, are due less to the peculiarities of their own minds than to the peculiarity of the moral and intellectual condition of the minds among which they have been produced. Thus a number of writers possess the form, whilst they want the spirit of those whom, it is alleged, they imitate; because the former is the endowment of the age in which they live, and the latter must be the uncommunicated lightning of their own mind.

The peculiar style of intense and comprehensive imagery which distinguishes the modern literature of England, has not been, as a general power, the product of the imitation of any particular writer. The mass of capabilities remains at every period materially the same; the circumstances which awaken it to action perpetually change. If England were divided into forty republics, each equal in population and extent to Athens, there is no reason to suppose but that, under institutions not more perfect than those of Athens, each would produce philosophers and poets equal to those who (if we except Shakespeare) have never been surpassed. We owe the great writers of the golden age of our literature to that fervid awakening of the public mind which shook to dust the oldest and most oppressive form of the Christian religion. We owe Milton to the progress and development of the same spirit: the sacred Milton was, let it ever be remembered, a republican, and a bold inquirer into morals and religion. The great writers of our own age are, we have reason to suppose, the companions and forerunners of some unimagined change in our social condition, or the opinions which cement it. The cloud of mind is discharging its collected lightning, and the equilibrium between institutions and opinions is now restoring, or is about to be restored.

As to imitation, poetry is a mimetic art. It creates, but it creates by combination and representation. Poetical abstractions are beautiful and new, not because the portions of which they are composed had no previous existence in the mind of man, or in nature, but because the whole produced by their combination has some intelligible and beautiful analogy with those sources of emotion and thought, and with the contemporary condition of them: one great poet is a masterpiece of nature, which another not only ought to study but must study. He might as wisely and as easily determine that his mind should no longer be the mirror of all that is lovely in the visible universe, as exclude from his contemplation the beautiful which exists in the writings of a great contemporary. The pretence of doing it would be a presumption in any but the greatest; the effect even in him, would be strained, unnatural, and ineffectual. A poet is the combined product of such internal powers as modify the nature of others; and of such external influences as excite and sustain these powers; he is not one, but both. Every man's mind is, in this respect, modified by all the objects of nature and art; by every word and every suggestion which he ever admitted to act upon his consciousness; it is the mirror upon which all forms are reflected, and in which they compose one form. Poets, not otherwise than philosophers, painters, sculptors, and musicians, are, in one sense, the creators, and, in another, the creations, of their age. From this subjection the loftiest do not escape. There is a similarity between Homer and Hesiod, between Æschylus and Euripides, between Virgil and Horace, between Dante and Petrarch, between Shakespeare and Fletcher, between Dryden and Pope; each has a generic resemblance under which their specific distinctions are arranged. If this similarity be the result of imitation, I am willing to confess that I have imitated.

Let this opportunity be conceded to me of acknowledging that I have, what a Scotch philosopher characteristically terms, "a passion for reforming the world:" what passion incited him to write and publish his book, he omits to explain. For my part, I had rather be damned with Plato and Lord Bacon, than to go to heaven with Paley and Malthus. But it is a mistake to suppose that I dedicate my poetical compositions solely to the direct enforcement of reform, or that I consider them in any degree as containing a reasoned system on the theory of human life. Didactic poetry is my abhorrence; nothing can be equally well expressed in prose that is not tedious and supererogatory in verse. My purpose has hitherto been simply to familiarise the highly refined imagination of the more select classes of poetical readers with beautiful idealisms of moral excellence; aware that until the mind can love, and admire, and trust, and hope, and endure, reasoned principles of moral conduct are seeds cast upon the highway of life, which the unconscious passenger tramples into dust, although they would bear the harvest of his happiness. Should I live to accomplish what I purpose, that is, produce a systematical history of what appear to me to be the genuine elements of human society, let not the advocates of injustice and superstition flatter themselves that I should take Æschylus rather than Plato as my model.

The having spoken of myself with unaffected freedom will need little apology with the candid; and let the uncandid consider that they injure me less than their own hearts and minds by misrepresentation. Whatever talents a person may possess to amuse and instruct others, be they ever so inconsiderable, he is yet bound to exert them: if his attempt be ineffectual, let the punishment of an unaccomplished purpose have been sufficient; let none trouble themselves to heap the dust of oblivion upon his efforts; the pile they raise will betray his grave, which might otherwise have been unknown.

SIR WALTER SCOTT
THE LADY OF THE LAKE
1810
Epilogue

HARP of the North, farewell! The hills grow dark,
  On purple peaks a deeper shade descending;
In twilight copse the glow-worm lights her spark,
  The deer, half-seen, are to the covert wending.
Resume thy wizard elm! the fountain lending
  And the wild breeze, thy wilder minstrelsy;
Thy numbers sweet with nature's vespers blending,
  With distant echo from the fold and lea,
And herd-boy's evening pipe, and hum of housing bee.

Yet once again, farewell, thou Minstrel harp!
  Yet, once again, forgive my feeble sway,
And little reck I of the censure sharp
  May idly cavil at an idle lay.
Much have I owed thy strain on life's long way,
  Through secret woes the world has never known,
When on the weary night dawn'd wearier day,
  And bitterer was the grief devour'd alone.
That I o'erlive such woes, Enchantress! is thine own.

Hark! as my lingering footsteps slow retire,
  Some Spirit of the Air has waked thy string!
'Tis now a seraph bold, with touch of fire,
  'Tis now the brush of Fairy's frolic wing.
Receding now, the dying numbers ring
  Fainter and fainter down the rugged dell,
And now the mountain breezes scarcely bring
  A wandering witch-note of the distant spell—
And now 'tis silent all!—Enchantress fare thee well!

SIR WALTER SCOTT

THE FORTUNES OF NIGEL

1822

Introductory Epistle

CAPTAIN.—But allowing, my dear sir, that you care not for your personal reputation, or for that of any literary person upon whose shoulders your faults may be visited, allow me to say, that common gratitude to the public, which has received you so kindly, and to the critics, who have treated you so leniently, ought to induce you to bestow more pains on your story.

Author.—I do entreat you, my son, as Dr Johnson would have said, "free your mind from cant." For the critics, they have their business, and I mine; as the nursery proverb goes—

> *The children in Holland take pleasure in making*
> *What the children in England take pleasure in breaking.*

I am their humble jackal, too busy providing food for them, to have time for considering whether they swallow or reject it.—To the public, I stand pretty nearly in the relation of the postman who leaves a packet at the door of an individual. If it contains pleasing intelligence, a billet from a mistress, a letter from an absent son, a remittance from a correspondent supposed to be bankrupt,—the letter is acceptably welcome, and read and re-read, folded up, filed, and safely deposited in the bureau. If the contents are disagreeable, if it comes from a dun or from a bore, the correspondent is cursed, the letter is thrown into the fire, and the expense of postage is heartily regretted; while all the time the bearer of the despatches is, in either case, as little thought on as the snow of last Christmas. The utmost extent of kindness between the author and the public which can really exist, is, that the world are disposed to be somewhat indulgent to the succeeding works of an original favourite, were it but on account of the habit which the public mind had acquired; while the author very naturally thinks well of *their* taste, who have so liberally applauded *his* productions. But I deny there is any call for gratitude, properly so called, either on one side or the other.

Captain.—Respect to yourself, then, ought to teach caution.

Author.—Ay, if caution could augment the chance of my success. But to confess to you the truth, the works and passages in which I have succeeded, have uniformly been written with the greatest rapidity; and when I have seen some of these placed in opposition with others, and commended as more highly finished, I could appeal to pen and standish, that the parts in which I have come feebly off, were by much the more laboured. Besides, I doubt the beneficial effect of too much delay, both on account of the author and the public. A man should strike while the iron is hot, and hoist sail while the wind is fair. If a successful author keep not the stage, another instantly takes his ground. If a writer lie by for ten years ere he produces a second work, he is superseded by others; or if the age is so poor of genius that this does not happen, his own reputation becomes his great obstacle. The public will expect the new work to be ten times better than its predecessor; the author will expect it should be ten times more popular, and 'tis a hundred to ten that both are disappointed.

Captain.—This may justify a certain degree of rapidity in publication, but not that which is proverbially said to be no speed. You should take time at least to arrange your story.

Author.—That is a sore point with me, my son. Believe me, I have not been fool enough to neglect ordinary precautions. I have repeatedly laid down my future work to scale, divided it into volumes and chapters, and endeavoured to construct a story which I meant should evolve itself gradually and strikingly, maintain suspense, and stimulate curiosity; and which, finally, should terminate in a striking catastrophe. But I think there is a demon who seats himself on the feather of my pen when I begin to write, and leads it astray from the purpose. Characters expand under my hand; incidents are multiplied; the story lingers, while the materials increase; my regular mansion turns out a Gothic anomaly, and the work is closed long before I have attained the point I had proposed.

Captain.—Resolution and determined forbearance might remedy that evil.

Author.—Alas! my dear sir, you do not know the force of paternal affection. When I light on such a character as Bailie Jarvie, or Dalgetty, my imagination brightens, and my conception becomes clearer at every step which I take in his company, although it leads me many a weary mile away from the regular road, and forces me to leap hedge and ditch to get back into the route again. If I resist the temptation, as you advise me, my thoughts become prosy, flat, and dull; I write painfully to myself, and under a consciousness of flagging which makes me flag still more; the sunshine with which fancy had invested the incidents, departs from them, and leaves every thing dull and gloomy. I am not more the same author I was in my better mood, than the dog in a wheel, condemned to go round and round for hours, is like the same dog merrily chasing his own tail, and gambolling in all the frolic of unrestrained freedom. In short, sir, on such occasions, I think I am bewitched. . . .

Captain.—You are determined to proceed then in your own system? Are you aware that an unworthy motive may be assigned for this rapid succession of publication? You will be supposed to work merely for the lucre of gain.

Author.—Supposing that I did permit the great advantages which must be derived from success in literature, to join with other motives in inducing me to come more frequently before the public, —that emolument is the voluntary tax which the public pays for a certain species of literary amusement—it is extorted from no one, and paid, I presume, by those only who can afford it, and who receive gratification in proportion to the expense. If the capital sum which these volumes have put into circulation be a very large one, has it contributed to my indulgence only? or can I not say to hundreds, from honest Duncan the paper manufacturer, to the most snivelling of the printer's devils, "Didst thou not share? Hadst thou not fifteen pence?" I profess I think our Modern Athens much obliged to me for having established such an extensive manufacture; and when universal suffrage comes in fashion, I intend to stand for a seat in the House on the interest of all the unwashed artificers connected with literature.

Captain.—This would be called the language of a calico manufacturer.

Author.—Cant again, my dear son—there is lime in this sack, too—nothing but sophistication in this world! I do say, in spite of Adam Smith and his followers, that a successful author is a productive labourer, and that his works constitute as effectual a part of the public wealth, as that which is created by any other manufacture. . . . I speak with reference to the diffusion of the wealth arising to the public, and the degree of industry which even such a trifling work as the present must stimulate and reward, before the volume leave the publisher's shop. Without me it could not exist, and to this extent I am a benefactor to the country. As for my own emolument, it is won by toil, and I account myself answerable to Heaven only for the mode in which I expend it. The candid may hope it is not all dedicated to selfish purposes, and without much pretensions to merit in him who disburses it, a part may "wander, heaven directed, to the poor."

Captain.—Yet it is generally held base to write from the mere motives of gain.

Author.—It would be base to do so exclusively, or even to make it a principal motive for literary exertion. Nay, I will venture to say that no work of imagination, proceeding from the mere consideration of a certain sum of copy-money, ever did, or ever will, succeed. . . . But no man of honour, genius, or spirit, would make the mere love of gain the chief, far less the only, purpose of his labours. For myself, I am not displeased to find the game a winning one; yet while I please the public, I should probably continue it merely for the pleasure of playing; for I have felt as strongly as most folks that love of composition, which is perhaps the strongest of all instincts, driving the author to the pen, the painter to the pallet, often without either the chance of fame or the prospect of reward. Perhaps I have said too much of this. I might, perhaps, with as much truth as most people, exculpate myself from the charge of being either of a greedy or mercenary disposition; but I am not, therefore, hypocrite enough to disclaim the ordinary motives, on account of which the whole world around me is toiling unremittingly, to the sacrifice of ease, comfort, health, and life. I do not affect the disinterestedness of that ingenuous association of gentlemen mentioned by Goldsmith, who sold their magazine for sixpence a-piece, merely for their own amusement. . . .

Captain.—You are willing then to barter future reputation for present popularity?

Author.—*Meliora spero.* Horace himself expected not to survive in all his works—I may hope to live in some of mine;—*non omnis moriar.*

THOMAS LOVE PEACOCK

Preface to

HEADLONG HALL

AND THE THREE NOVELS PUBLISHED ALONG WITH IT

1837

ALL these little publications appeared originally without prefaces. I left them to speak for themselves; and I thought I might very fitly preserve my own impersonality, having never intruded on the personality of others, nor taken any liberties but with public conduct and public opinions. But an old friend assures me, that to publish a book without a preface is like entering a drawing-room without making a bow. In deference to this opinion, though I am not quite clear of its soundness, I make my prefatory bow at this eleventh hour.

"Headlong Hall" was written in 1815; "Nightmare Abbey," in 1817; "Maid Marian," with the exception of the last three chapters, in 1818; "Crotchet Castle," in 1830. I am desirous to note the intervals, because, at each of those periods, things were true, in great matters and in small, which are true no longer. "Headlong Hall" begins with the Holyhead Mail, and "Crotchet Castle" ends with a rotten borough. The Holyhead Mail no longer keeps the same hours, nor stops at the Capel Cerig Inn, which the progress of improvement has thrown out of the road; and the rotten boroughs of 1830 have ceased to exist, though there are some very pretty pocket properties, which are their worthy successors. But the classes of tastes, feelings, and opinions, which were successively brought into play in these little tales, remain substantially the same. Perfectibilians, deteriorationists, statu-quo-ites, phrenologists, transcendentalists, political economists, theorists in all sciences, projectors in all arts, morbid visionaries, romantic enthusiasts, lovers of music, lovers of the picturesque, and lovers of good dinners, march, and will march for ever, *pari passu* with the march of mechanics, which some facetiously call the march of intellect. The fastidious in old wine are a race that does not decay. Literary violaters of the confidences of private life still gain a disreputable livelihood and an unenviable notoriety. Match-makers from interest, and the disappointed in love and in friendship, are varieties of which specimens are extant. The great principle of the Right of Might is as flourishing now as in the days of Maid Marian: the array of false pretensions, moral, political, and literary, is as imposing as ever: the rulers of the world still feel things in their effects, and never foresee them in their causes: and political mountebanks continue, and will continue, to puff nostrums and practise legerdemain under the eyes of the multitude: following, like the "learned friend" of Crotchet Castle, a course as tortuous as that of a river, but in a reverse process; beginning by being dark and deep, and ending by being transparent.

THE AUTHOR OF "HEADLONG HALL"

March 4, 1837.

THE REV. SYDNEY SMITH

WORKS

1839

Preface

WHEN first I went into the Church, I had a curacy in the middle of Salisbury Plain. The Squire of the parish took a fancy to me, and asked me to go with his son to reside at the University of Weimar: before we could get there Germany became the seat of war, and in stress of politics we put into Edinburgh, where I remained five years. The principles of the French Revolution were then fully afloat, and it is impossible to conceive a more violent and agitated state of society. Among the first persons with whom I am acquainted were, Lord Jeffrey, Lord Murray (late Lord Advocate for Scotland), and Lord Brougham: all of them maintaining opinions upon political subjects a little too liberal for the dynasty of Dundas, then exercising supreme power over the northern division of the island.

One day we happened to meet in the eighth or ninth story or flat in Buccleugh-place, the elevated residence of the then Mr. Jeffrey. I proposed that we should set up a Review; this was acceded to with acclamations. I was appointed Editor, and remained long enough in Edinburgh to edit the first number of the Edinburgh Review. The motto I proposed for the Review was,

"*Tenui musam meditamur avena.*"
"We cultivate literature upon a little oatmeal."

But this was too near the truth to be admitted, so we took our present grave motto from *Publius Syrus*, of whom none of us had, I am sure, ever read a single line; and so began what has since turned out to be a very important and able journal. When I left Edinburgh, it fell into the stronger hands of Lord Jeffrey and Lord Brougham, and reached the highest point of popularity and success.

I contributed from England many articles, which I have been foolish enough to collect, and publish with some other tracts written by me.

To appreciate the value of the Edinburgh Review, the state of England at the period when that journal began should be had in remembrance. The Catholics were not emancipated—the Corporation and Test Acts were unrepealed—the Game Laws were horribly oppressive—Steel Traps and Spring Guns were set all over the country—Prisoners tried for their Lives could have no Counsel —Lord Eldon and the Court of Chancery pressed heavily upon mankind—Libel was punished by the most cruel and vindictive imprisonments—the principles of Political Economy were little understood—the Law of Debt and of Conspiracy were upon the worst possible footing—the enormous wickedness of the Slave Trade was tolerated—a thousand evils were in existence, which the talents of good and able men have since lessened or removed; and these effects have been not a little assisted by the honest boldness of the Edinburgh Review.

I see very little in my Reviews to alter or repent of; I always endeavoured to fight against evil; and what I thought evil then, I think evil now. I am heartily glad that all our disqualifying laws for religious opinions are abolished, and I see nothing in such measures but unmixed good and real increase of strength to our Establishment. . . . From the beginning of the century (about which time the Review began) to the death of Lord Liverpool, was an awful period for those who had the misfortune to entertain liberal opinions, and who were too honest to sell them for the ermine of the judge, or the lawn of the prelate:—a long and hopeless career in your profession, the chuckling grin of noodles, the sarcastic leer of the genuine political rogue—prebendaries, deans, and bishops made over your head—reverend renegadoes advanced to the highest dignities of the Church for helping to rivet the fetters of Catholic and Protestant Dissenters, and no more chance of a Whig administration than of a thaw in Zembla—these were the penalties exacted for liberality of opinion at that period; and not only was there no pay, but there were many stripes. It is always considered as a piece of impertinence in England, if a man of less than two or three thousand a year has any opinions at all upon important subjects; and in addition he was sure at that time to be assailed with all the Billingsgate of the French Revolution—Jacobin, Leveller, Atheist, Deist, Socinian, Incendiary, Regicide, were the gentlest appellations used; and the man who breathed a syllable against the senseless bigotry of the two Georges or hinted at the abominable tyranny and persecution exercised upon Catholic Ireland, was shunned as unfit for the relations of social life. Not a murmur against any abuse was permitted; to say a word against the suitorcide delays of the Court of Chancery, or the cruel punishments of the Game Laws, or against any abuse which a rich man inflicted or a poor man suffered, was treason against the *Plousiocracy* and was bitterly and steadily resented. Lord Gray had not then taken off the bearing-rein from the English people, as Sir Francis Head has now done from horses.

To set on foot such a Journal in such times, to contribute towards it for many years, to bear patiently the reproach and poverty which it caused, and to look back and see that I have nothing to retract, and no intemperance and violence to reproach myself with, is a career of life which I must think to be extremely fortunate. Strange and ludicrous are the changes in human affairs. The Tories are now on the treadmill, and the well-paid Whigs are riding in chariots: with many faces, however, looking out of the windows (including that of our Prime Minister,) which I never remember to have seen in the days of the poverty and depression of Whiggism. Liberality is now a lucrative business. Whoever has any institution to destroy, may consider himself as a commissioner, and his fortune as made; and, to my utter and never-ending astonishment, I, an old Edinburgh Reviewer, find myself fighting, in the year 1839, against the Archbishop of Canterbury and the Bishop of London, for the existence of the National Church.

SYDNEY SMITH.

June 1839.

WILLIAM MAKEPEACE THACKERAY

THE HISTORY OF
PENDENNIS

1850

Preface

IF this kind of composition, of which the two years' product is now laid before the public, fail in art, as it constantly does and must, it at least has the advantage of a certain truth and honesty, which a work more elaborate might lose. In his constant communication with the reader, the writer is forced into frankness of expression, and to speak out his own mind and feelings as they urge him. Many a slip of the pen and the printer, many a word spoken in haste, he sees and would recall as he looks over his volume. It is a sort of confidential talk between writer and reader, which must often be dull, must often flag. In the course of his volubility, the perpetual speaker must of necessity lay bare his own weaknesses, vanities, peculiarities. And as we judge of a man's character, after long frequenting his society, not by one speech, or by one mood or opinion, or by one day's talk, but by the tenor of his general bearing and conversation; so of a writer, who delivers himself up to you perforce unreservedly, you say, Is he honest? Does he tell the truth in the main? Does he seem actuated by a desire to find out and speak it? Is he a quack, who shams sentiment, or mouths for effect? Does he seek popularity by claptraps or other arts? I can no more ignore good fortune than any other chance which has befallen me. I have found many thousands more readers than I ever looked for. I have no right to say to these, You shall not find fault with my art, or fall asleep over my pages; but I ask you to believe that this person writing strives to tell the truth. If there is not that, there is nothing.

Perhaps the lovers of "excitement" may care to know, that this book began with a very precise plan, which was entirely put aside.

Ladies and gentlemen, you were to have been treated, and the writer's and the publisher's pocket benefited, by the recital of the most active horrors. What more exciting than a ruffian (with many admirable virtues) in St. Giles's visited constantly by a young lady from Belgravia? What more stirring than the contrasts of society? the mixture of slang and fashionable language? the escapes, the battles, the murders? Nay, up to nine o'clock this very morning, my poor friend, Colonel Altamont, was doomed to execution, and the author only relented when his victim was actually at the window.

The "exciting" plan was laid aside (with a very honourable forbearance on the part of the publishers) because, on attempting it, I found that I failed from want of experience of my subject; and never having been intimate with any convict in my life, and the manners of ruffians and gaol-birds being quite unfamiliar to me, the idea of entering into competition with M. Eugène Sue was abandoned. To describe a real rascal, you must make him so horrible that he would be too hideous to show; and unless the painter paints him fairly, I hold he has no right to show him at all.

Even the gentlemen of our age—this is an attempt to describe one of them, no better nor worse than most educated men—even these we cannot show as they are, with the notorious foibles and selfishness of their lives and their education. Since the author of "Tom Jones" was buried, no writer of fiction among us has been permitted to depict to his utmost power a MAN. We must drape him, and give him a certain conventional simper. Society will not tolerate the Natural in our Art. Many ladies have remonstrated and subscribers left me, because, in the course of the story, I described a young man resisting and affected by temptation. My object was to say, that he had the passions to feel, and the manliness and generosity to overcome them. You will not hear—it is best to know it—what moves in the real world, what passes in society, in the clubs, colleges, mess-rooms,—what is the life and talk of your sons. A little more frankness than is customary has been attempted in this story; with no bad desire on the writer's part, it is hoped, and with no ill consequence to any reader. If truth is not always pleasant, at any rate truth is best, from whatever chair—from those whence graver writers or thinkers argue, as from that at which the story-teller sits as he concludes his labour, and bids his kind reader farewell.

KENSINGTON:

Nov. 26th, 1850.

ANTHONY TROLLOPE

THE LAST CHRONICLE OF BARSET
1867

Conclusion

. . . BEFORE I take my leave of the diocese of Barchester for ever,
which I purpose to do in the succeeding paragraph, I desire to be
allowed to say one word of apology for myself, in answer to those
who have accused me,—always without bitterness, and generally
with tenderness,—of having forgotten, in writing of clergymen, the
first and most prominent characteristic of the ordinary English
clergyman's life. I have described many clergymen, they say, but
have spoken of them all as though their professional duties, their
high calling, their daily workings for the good of those around
them, were matters of no moment, either to me, or, in my opinion,
to themselves. I would plead, in answer to this, that my object
has been to paint the social and not the professional lives of clergymen; and that I have been led to do so, firstly, by a feeling that as
no men affect more strongly, by their own character, the society
of those around than do country clergymen, so, therefore, their
social habits have been worth the labour necessary for painting
them; and secondly, by a feeling that though I, as a novelist, may
feel myself entitled to write of clergymen out of their pulpits, as I
may also write of lawyers and doctors, I have no such liberty to
write of them in their pulpits. When I have done so, if I have
done so, I have so far transgressed. There are those who have
told me that I have made all my clergymen bad, and none good.
I must venture to hint to such judges that they have taught their
eyes to love a colouring higher than nature justifies. We are,
most of us, apt to love Raphael's madonnas better than Rembrandt's
matrons. But, though we do so, we know that Rembrandt's
matrons existed; but we do have a strong belief that no such woman
as Raphael painted ever did exist. In that he painted, as he may
be surmised to have done, for pious purposes,—at least for Church

purposes,—Raphael was justified; but had he painted so for family portraiture he would have been false.   Had I written an epic about clergymen, I would have taken St. Paul for my model; but describing, as I have endeavoured to do, such clergymen as I see around me, I could not venture to be transcendental.   For myself I can only say that I shall always be happy to sit, when allowed to do so, at the table of Archdeacon Grantly, to walk through the High Street of Barchester arm in arm with Mr. Robarts of Framley, and to stand alone and shed a tear beneath the modest black stone in the north transept of the cathedral on which is inscribed the name of Septimus Harding.

And now, if the reader will allow me to seize him affectionately by the arm, we will together take our last farewell of Barset and of the towers of Barchester.   I may not venture to say to him that, in this country, he and I together have wandered often through the country lanes, and have ridden together over the too-well wooded fields, or have stood together in the cathedral nave listening to the peals of the organ, or have together sat at good men's tables, or have confronted together the angry pride of men who were not good.   I may not boast that any beside myself have so realized the place, and the people, and the facts, as to make such reminiscences possible as those which I should attempt to evoke by an appeal to perfect fellowship.   But to me Barset has been a real county, and its city a real city, and the spires and towers have been before my eyes, and the voices of the people are known to my ears, and the pavement of the city ways are familiar to my footsteps.   To them all I now say farewell.   That I have been induced to wander among them too long by my love of old friendships, and by the sweetness of old faces, is a fault for which I may perhaps be more readily forgiven, when I repeat, with some solemnity of assurance, the promise made in my title, that this shall be the last chronicle of Barset.

WILLIAM MORRIS
THE EARTHLY PARADISE
1868
An Apology

OF Heaven or Hell I have no power to sing,
I cannot ease the burden of your fears,
Or make quick-coming death a little thing,
Or bring again the pleasure of past years,
Nor for my words shall ye forget your tears,
Or hope again for aught that I can say,
The idle singer of an empty day.

But rather, when aweary of your mirth,
From full hearts still unsatisfied ye sigh,
And feeling kindly unto all the earth,
Grudge every minute as it passes by,
Made the more mindful that the sweet days die—
—Remember me a little then I pray,
The idle singer of an empty day.

The heavy trouble, the bewildering care
That weighs us down who live and earn our bread,
These idle verses have no power to bear;
So let me sing of names remembered,
Because they, living not, can ne'er be dead,
Or long time take their memory quite away
From us poor singers of an empty day.

Dreamer of dreams, born out of my due time,
Why should I strive to set the crooked straight?
Let it suffice me that my murmuring rhyme
Beats with light wing against the ivory gate,

Telling a tale not too importunate
To those who in the sleepy region stay,
Lulled by the singer of an empty day.

Folk say, a wisard to a northern king
At Christmas-tide such wondrous things did show,
That through one window men beheld the spring,
And through another saw the summer glow,
And through a third the fruited vines a-row,
While still, unheard, but in its wonted way,
Piped the drear wind of that December day.

So with this Earthly Paradise it is,
If ye will read aright, and pardon me,
Who strive to build a shadowy isle of bliss
Midmost the beating of the steely sea,
Where tossed about all hearts of men must be;
Whose ravening monsters mighty men shall slay,
Not the poor singer of an empty day.

GEORGE ELIOT

MIDDLEMARCH
1872

Prelude

WHO that cares much to know the history of man, and how the
mysterious mixture behaves under the varying experiments of
Time, has not dwelt, at least briefly, on the life of Saint Theresa,
has not smiled with some gentleness at the thought of the little
girl walking forth one morning hand-in-hand with her still smaller
brother, to go and seek martyrdom in the country of the Moors?
Out they toddled from rugged Avila, wide-eyed and helpless-
looking as two fawns, but with human hearts, already beating to a
national idea; until domestic reality met them in the shape of uncles,
and turned them back from their great resolve. That child-
pilgrimage was a fit beginning. Theresa's passionate, ideal nature
demanded an epic life: what were many-volumed romances of
chivalry and the social conquests of a brilliant girl to her? Her
flame quickly burned up that light fuel; and, fed from within,
soared after some illimitable satisfaction, some object which would
never justify weariness, which would reconcile self-despair with the
rapturous consciousness of life beyond self. She found her epos in
the reform of a religious order.

That Spanish woman who lived three hundred years ago, was
certainly not the last of her kind. Many Theresas have been born
who found for themselves no epic life wherein there was a constant
unfolding of far-resonant action; perhaps only a life of mistakes,
the offspring of a certain spiritual grandeur ill-matched with the
meanness of opportunity; perhaps a tragic failure which found no
sacred poet and sank unwept into oblivion. With dim lights and
tangled circumstance they tried to shape their thought and deed
in noble agreement; but after all, to common eyes their struggles
seemed mere inconsistency and formlessness; for these later-born
Theresas were helped by no coherent social faith and order which

could perform the function of knowledge for their ardently willing soul. Their ardour alternated between a vague ideal and the common yearning of womanhood; so that the one was disapproved as extravagance, and the other condemned as a lapse.

Some have felt that these blundering lives are due to the inconvenient indefiniteness with which the Supreme Power has fashioned the natures of women: if there were one level of feminine incompetence as strict as the ability to count three and no more, the social lot of women might be treated with scientific certitude. Meanwhile the indefiniteness remains, and the limits of variations are really much wider than anyone would imagine from the sameness of women's coiffure and the favourite love-stories in prose and verse. Here and there a cygnet is reared uneasily among the ducklings in the brown pond, and never finds the living stream in fellowship with its own oary-footed kind. Here and there is born a Saint Theresa, foundress of nothing, whose loving heart-beats and sobs after an unattained goodness tremble off and are dispersed among hindrances, instead of centering in some long-recognisable deed.

ROBERT LOUIS STEVENSON
VIRGINIBUS PUERISQUE
1881
Dedication

My Dear William Ernest Henley,

    We are all busy in this world building Towers of Babel; and the child of our imaginations is always a changeling when it comes from nurse. This is not only true in the greatest, as of wars and folios, but in the least also, like the trifling volume in your hand. Thus I began to write these papers with a definite end: I was to be the *Advocatus*, not I hope *Diaboli*, but *Juventutis*. I was to state temperately the beliefs of youth as opposed to the contentions of age; to go over all the field where the two differ, and produce at last a little volume of special pleadings which I might call, without misnomer, "Life at Twenty-five." But times kept changing, and I shared in the change. I clung hard to that entrancing age; but, with the best will, no man can be twenty-five for ever. The old, ruddy convictions deserted me, and, along with them, the style that fits their presentation and defence. I saw, and indeed my friends informed me, that the game was up. A good part of the volume would answer to the long-projected title; but the shadows of the prison-house are on the rest.

It is good to have been young in youth and, as years go on, to grow older. Many are already old before they are through their teens; but to travel deliberately through one's ages is to get the heart out of a liberal education. Times change, opinions vary to their opposite, and still this world appears a brave gymnasium, full of sea-bathing, and horse exercise, and bracing, manly virtues; and what can be more encouraging than to find the friend who was welcome at one age, still welcome at another? Our affections and beliefs are wiser than we; the best that is in us is better than we can understand; for it is grounded beyond experience, and guides us, blindfold but safe from one age on to another.

These papers are like milestones on the wayside of my life; and as I look back in memory, there is hardly a stage of that distance but I see you present with advice, reproof, or praise.   Meanwhile, many things have changed, you and I among the rest; but I hope that our sympathy, founded on the love of our art, and nourished by mutual assistance, shall survive these little revolutions undiminished, and, with God's help, unite us to the end.

R. L. S.

Davos Platz, 1881.

COVENTRY PATMORE

POEMS
1886

Preface to the Second Collective Edition

WITH this reprint I believe that I am closing my task as a poet, having traversed the ground and reached the end which, in my youth, I saw before me.   I have written little, but it is all my best; I have never spoken when I had nothing to say, nor spared time or labour to make my words true.   I have respected posterity; and, should there be a posterity which cares for letters, I dare to hope that it will respect me.

C. P.

HASTINGS, 1886.

MATTHEW ARNOLD

IRISH ESSAYS

1882

Preface

THE Essays which make the chief part of this volume have all
appeared during the last year or two in well-known periodicals.
The Prefaces which follow at the end were published in 1853 and
1854 as prefaces to my *Poems*, and have not been reprinted since.
Some of the readers of my poetry have expressed a wish for their
reappearance, and with that wish I here comply. Exactly as they
stand, I should not have written them now; but perhaps they are
none the worse on that account.

The three essays regarding Ireland which commence the present
volume, and which give it its title, were received with no great
favour when they appeared, and will probably be received with no
great favour now. Practical politicians and men of the world are
apt rather to resent the incursion of a man of letters into the field
of politics; he is, in truth, not on his own ground there, and is in
peculiar danger of talking at random. No one feels this more than
I do. Nevertheless I have set in the front of this volume the
essays on Irish affairs. If I am asked why, I should be disposed to
answer that I am curious to know how they will look ten years
hence, if anyone happens to turn to them.

English people keep asking themselves what we ought to do about
Ireland. The great contention of these essays is, that in order to
attach Ireland to us solidly, English people have not only to *do*
something different from what they have done hitherto, they have
also to *be* something different from what they have been hitherto.
As a whole as a community, they have to acquire a larger and
sweeter temper, a larger and more lucid mind. And this is indeed
no light task, yet it is the capital task now appointed to us and our
safety depends on our accomplishing it: to *be* something different,
much more, even, than to *do* something different. . . .

To heal the estrangement between Ireland and England is what is needed above all things, and I cannot say that the Land Act appears to me to have in itself the elements for healing it. Nor can I see the use of pretending to find them in it if they are not really there. Nothing, indeed, could be more absurd than for irresponsible people to press seriously their fancy solutions, though they may properly enough throw them out, on a suitable occasion, for purposes of discussion and illustration. Nothing, moreover, is further from my thoughts, in what is here said, than to find fault with the responsible Government, which has to provide not a fancy solution for difficulties, but a solution which may be put into practice. I know that it was as impossible to go on governing Ireland by means of the landlords as by means of the Protestant Church. I am ready to admit that the Government, the power and *purchase* at their disposal being what it is, could not well but have had recourse to some such measure as the Land Act. I think, even, as I have said in the following pages, that the Land Act of the Government, with what it does and what it gives the power of doing, is probably quite capable of satisfying the Irish people as a Land Act, if a certain other indispensable condition is complied with. But this condition the Land Act will not of itself realise. The indispensable condition is, that England and English civilisation shall become more attractive; or, as I began by saying, that we should not only *do* to Ireland something different from what we have done hitherto, but should also *be* something different. On this need of a changed and more attractive power in English civilisation almost all the essays in the present volume, and not alone those dealing directly with Ireland, will be found to insist.

The barren logomachies of Plato's *Theœtetus* are relieved by half a dozen immortal pages, and among them are those in which is described the helplessness of the philosopher in the ways of the world, the helplessness of the man of the world in a spiritual crisis. The philosopher Thales in the ditch had been an easy and a frequent subject for merriment; it was reserved for Plato to amuse himself with the practical politician and man of the world in a spiritual crisis. Mr. Jowett is uncommonly happy in his translation of

Plato's account of the man of the world, at such a crisis, "drawn into the upper air," having to "get himself out of his commonplaces to the consideration of government and of human happiness and misery in general,—what they are, and how a man is to attain the one and avoid the other." "Then, indeed," says Plato, "when that narrow, vain, little practical mind is called to account about all this, he gives the philosopher his revenge. For dizzied by the height at which he is hanging, whence he looks into space which is a strange experience to him, he being dismayed and lost and stammering out broken words is laughed at, not by Thracian handmaidens such as laughed at Thales, or by any other uneducated persons, for they have no eye for the situation, but by every man who has been brought up as a true freeman."

Our practical politicians and men of the world, carried up by the course of time and change into a new air, and still ruefully trying there to gasp out their formulas, such as "Freedom of contract" or "The Liberal party has emphatically condemned religious endowment," or "Our traditional, existing, social arrangements," could not be better hit off. The man of the world, with his utter astonishment that the Irish tenants should stop the hunting, when the hunting "caused the noble master of the hounds to spend among them ten thousand a year!" the man of the world, with his mournful and incessant cries of "Revolution!" Yes, we are in a revolution; "a revolution," as the late Duke of Wellington said, "by due course of law." And one of the features of it is, that the Irish tenants prefer to stop the hunting of those whom they regard as a set of aliens amongst them for sporting purposes, who have in the past treated them and spoken to them as if they were slaves, and who are disposed, many of them, to treat them and speak to them as if they were slaves still,—the Irish people had rather stop this hunting, than profit by an expenditure upon it to the tune of ten thousand a year. The man of the world has had and has one formula for attaching neighbours and tenants to us, and one only,—expenditure. And now he is "drawn into upper air," and has to hear such new and strange formulas as this, for example, of the most charming of French moralists:—*Pour gagner l'humanité, il faut lui plaire; pour lui plaire, il faut être aimable.* Or, if the man of the world can stand Holy Writ, let him hear the Psalmist:—"*Mansueti posside-bunt terram*, the gentle shall possess the earth."

Indeed we are at the end of a period, and always at the end of a period the word goes forth: "Now is the judgment of this world." The "traditional, existing, social arrangements," which satisfied before, satisfy no longer; the conventions and phrases, which once passed without question, are challenged. That saying of the saints comes to be fulfilled: *Peribit totum quod non est ex Deo ortum.* Each people has its own periods of national life, with their own characters. The period which is now ending for England is that which began, when, after the sensuous tumult of the Renascence, Catholicism being discredited and gone, our serious nation desired, as had been foretold, "to see one of the days of the Son of Man and did not see it"; but men said to them, *See here,* or *See there,* and they went after the blind guides and followed the false direction; and the actual civilisation of England and of America is the result. A civilisation with many virtues; but without lucidity of mind, and without largeness of temper. And now we English, at any rate, have to acquire them, and to learn the necessity for us "to live," as Emerson says, "from a greater depth of being." The sages and the saints alike have always preached this necessity; the so-called practical people and men of the world have always derided it. In the present collapse of their wisdom, we ought to find it less hard to rate their stock ideas and stock phrases, their claptrap and their catchwords, at their proper value, and to cast in our lot boldly with the sages and with the saints. *Sine ut mortui sepeliant mortuos suos, sed tu vade adnuntia regnum Dei.*

JOHN RUSKIN

MODERN PAINTERS

I

Preface to the First Edition

1842

1. THE work now laid before the public originated in indignation at the shallow and false criticisms of the periodicals of the day on the works of the great living artist to whom it principally refers. It was intended to be a short pamphlet, reprobating the manner and style of those critiques, and pointing out their perilous tendency, as guides of public feeling. But, as point after point presented itself for demonstration, I found myself compelled to amplify what was at first a letter to the editor of a Review, into something very like a treatise on art, to which I was obliged to give the more consistency and completeness, because it advocated opinions which, to the ordinary connoisseur, will sound heretical. I now scarcely know whether I should announce it as an Essay on Landscape Painting, and apologize . . . for its lengthy discussion of general principles. But of whatever character the work may be considered, the motives which led me to undertake it must not be mistaken. No zeal for the reputation of any individual, no personal feeling of any kind, has the slightest weight or influence with me. The reputation of the great artist to whose works I have chiefly referred, is established on too legitimate grounds among all whose admiration is honourable, to be in any way affected by the ignorant sarcasms of pretension and affectation. But when *public* taste seems plunging deeper and deeper into degradation day by day, and when the press universally exerts such power as it possesses to direct the feeling of the nation more completely to all that is theatrical, affected, and false in art; while it vents its ribaldry on the most exalted truth, and the highest ideal of landscape that this or any other age has ever witnessed, it becomes the imperative duty of all who have any perception or knowledge of what is really great in art, and any desire for its

advancement in England, to come fearlessly forward, regardless of such individual interests as are likely to be injured by the knowledge of what is good and right, to declare and demonstrate, wherever they exist, the essence and the authority of the Beautiful and the True.

2. Whatever may seem invidious or partial in the execution of my task is dependent not so much on the tenor of the work, as on its incompleteness. I have not entered into systematic criticism of all the painters of the present day; but I have illustrated each particular excellence and truth of art by the works in which it exists in the highest degree, resting satisfied that if it be once rightly felt and enjoyed in these, it will be discovered and appreciated wherever it exists in others. And although I have never suppressed any conviction of the superiority of one artist over another, which I believed to be grounded on truth, and necessary to the understanding of truth, I have been cautious never to undermine positive rank, while I disputed relative rank. My uniform desire and aim have been, not that the present favourite should be admired less, but that the neglected master should be admired more. And I know that an increased perception and sense of truth and beauty, though it may interfere with our estimate of the comparative rank of painters, will invariably tend to increase our admiration of all who are really great; and he who now places Stanfield and Callcott above Turner, will admire Stanfield and Callcott more than he does now, when he has learned to place Turner far above them both.

3.   .   .   .   .   .

Of the old masters I have spoken with far greater freedom; but let it be remembered that only a portion of the work is now presented to the public, and it must not be supposed, because in that particular portion, and with reference to particular excellences, I have spoken in constant depreciation, that I have no feeling of other excellences of which cognizance can only be taken in future parts of the work. Let me not be understood to mean more than I have said, nor be made responsible for conclusions when I have only stated facts. I have said that the old masters did not give the truth of nature; if the reader chooses, thence, to infer that they were not masters at all, it is his conclusion, not mine.

4. Whatever I have asserted throughout the work, I have endeavoured to ground altogether on demonstrations which must stand or fall by their own strength, and which ought to involve no more reference to authority or character than a demonstration in Euclid. Yet it is proper for the public to know that the writer is no mere theorist, but has been devoted from his youth to the laborious study of practical art.

Whatever has been generally affirmed of the old schools of landscape painting is founded on familiar acquaintance with every important work of art, from Antwerp to Naples. But it would be useless, where close and immediate comparison with works in our own Academy is desirable, to refer to the details of pictures at Rome or Munich; and it would be impossible to speak at once with just feeling, as regarded the possessor, and just freedom, as regarded the public, of pictures in private galleries. Whatever particular references have been made for illustration have been therefore confined, as far as was in my power, to works in the National and Dulwich Galleries.

5. Finally, I have to apologize for the imperfection of a work which I could have wished not to have executed but with years of reflection and revisal. It is owing to my sense of the necessity of such revisal, that only a portion of the work is now presented to the public; but that portion is both complete in itself, and is more peculiarly directed against the crying evil which called for instant remedy. Whether I ever completely fulfil my intention will partly depend upon the spirit in which the present volume is received. If it be attributed to an invidious spirit, or a desire for the advancement of individual interests, I could hope to effect little good by farther effort. If, on the contrary, its real feeling and intention be understood, I shall shrink from no labour in the execution of a task which may tend, however feebly, to the advancement of the cause of real art in England, and to the honour of those great living Masters whom we now neglect or malign, to pour our flattery into the ear of Death, and exalt, with vain acclamation, the names of those who neither demand our praise, nor regard our gratitude.

THE AUTHOR.

II

From the Epilogue of

1883

12. In September, Mr. J. D. Harding, who, after Copley Fielding, had been my master in water-colour, wrote to ask if he could join me in his autumn tour. I went down to meet him at Baveno; and thence we drove quietly in an open carriage by Como and the spurs of the Italian Alps to Venice, walking up all the hills, stopping at all the river sides, sleeping a night or two at Como, Bergamo, Brescia, and Padua,—with a week at Verona. A most happy time, for me; and, I believe, for us both.

Harding had vivid, healthy, and unerring artistic faculty, but no depth of science, and scarcely any of sentiment. I saw him once impressed by the desolation of the great hall of the Casa Foscari; but in general, if the forms of the subject were picturesque, it was all he cared for, nor would he with any patience analyze even those. So far as his art and aim went, I was able entirely to sympathize with him; and we both liked, in one way or another, exactly the same sorts of things; so that he didn't want to go and draw the marshes at Mantua when I wanted to draw Monte Monterone—but we could always sit down to work within a dozen yards of each other, both pleased. I did not mind his laughing at me for poring into the foreground weeds, which he thought sufficiently expressed by a zigzag, and heartily admired in him the brilliancy of easy skill, which secured, and with emphasis, in an hour or two, the effect of scenes I could never have attempted.

His time in travelling was of course professionally too valuable to him to admit of much study in galleries, (which for the rest, when a painter's manner is once fixed, usually does him more hurt than good). But he generally went with me on my exploring days in Venice, and we saw the Scuola di San Rocco together, and both of us for the first time. My companion, though by no means modest as to his own powers, was (partly for that very reason, his confidence in them being well grounded) quite frank and candid in his admiration of stronger painters; and when we had got through the upper gallery, and into the room of the Crucifixion, we both sate down and looked—not at it—but at each other,—literally the strength so taken out of us that we couldn't stand:

When we came away, Harding said that he felt like a whipped schoolboy. I, not having been at school so long as he, felt only that a new world was opened to me, that I had seen that day the Art of Man in its full majesty for the first time; and that there was also a strange and precious gift in myself enabling me to recognize it, and therein ennobling, not crushing me. That sense of my own gift and function as an interpreter strengthened as I grew older; and supports, and I believe justifies me now in accepting in this last cycle of life, the responsibilities lately once more offered to me in Oxford.

13. The public estimate of me, so far as it is wise at all, and not grounded merely on my manner of writing, is, I think, chiefly as an illustrator of natural beauty. They had as much illustration of it before as they needed, one would have thought, and if not enough to their taste in Chaucer or Spenser, in Byron or Scott, at all events in their own contemporary poets. Tennyson's "Brook" is far beyond anything I ever did, or could have done, in beauty of description; and the entire power of natural scenes on the constant feelings of the human heart is taught, (and perfectly,) by Longfellow in "Hiawatha." But I say with pride, which it has become my duty to express openly, that it was left to me, and to me alone, first to discern, and then to teach, so far as in this hurried century any such thing *can* be taught, the excellency and supremacy of five great painters, despised until I spoke of them,—Turner, Tintoret, Luini, Botticelli, and Carpaccio. Despised,—nay, scarcely in any true sense of the word, known. I think, before the year 1874, in which I began work on the frescoes of Botticelli and Perugino in the Sistine Chapel, there will scarcely be found so much as a notice of their existence in the diary of any traveller, and there was no consciousness of their existence in the entire mind of modern Rome. They are little enough noticed *now*; and yet, in London, Turner's most precious drawings are kept in the cellar of the National

Gallery:—nevertheless, my work is done; and so far as the English nation studies the Arts at all, will tell, in its due time. . . .

III

Epilogue 1888

The republication of this book may seem to break faith with persons who have bought the old editions at advanced prices, trusting my announced resolution that no other should be issued during my lifetime.   Had I remained in active health, none could have been; for I should have employed the engravers otherwise, (especially Mr. Allen himself); but I have permitted the re-issue of this early work, to be of what use it may, finding that my plans of better things in the same direction must be abandoned.   For the rest, I never encourage the purchase, at advanced prices, of books which their authors wish to withdraw from circulation; and finally, I believe the early editions will never lose their value in the book-market, the original impressions of the plates by Mr. Armytage and Mr. Cousen being entirely beyond imitation by restored plates.   Mr. Allen's advertisements are trustworthy as to the cost and pains which have been given to bring the steels up to their first standard,[1] and the adequacy of the impressions obtained to answer the general purposes of the first engraving.   But no retouched plate is ever really worth the original one.

Although, as I have said, the book would not have been reprinted if I had been able to write a better to the same effect, I am glad, as matters stand, that the chapters in which I first eagerly and passionately said what throughout life I have been trying more earnestly and resolutely to say, should be put within the reach of readers who care to refer to them.

For the divisions of religious tenet and school to which I attached mistaken importance in my youth, do not in the least affect the vital teaching and purpose of this book: the claim, namely, of the

---

[1] This reference is to the plates of the large edition.

Personal relation of God to man as the source of all human, as distinguished from brutal, virtue and art. The assertion of this Personal character of God must be carefully and clearly distinguished by every reader who wishes to understand either "Modern Painters" or any of my more cautiously written subsequent books, from the statement of any Christian doctrine, as commonly accepted. I am always under the necessity of numbering with exactness, and frequently I can explain with sympathy, the articles of the Christian creed as it has been held by the various painters or writers of whose work I have to speak. But the religious faith on which my own art teaching is based never has been farther defined, nor have I wished to define it farther, than in the sentence beginning the theoretical part of "Modern Painters":—

"Man's use and purpose—and let the reader who will not grant me this, follow me no farther, for this I purpose always to assume—is to be the witness of the glory of God, and to advance that glory by his reasonable obedience and resultant happiness."

Nothing is here said of any tradition of Fall, or of any scheme of Redemption; nothing of Eternal Punishment, nothing of Immortal Life. It is assumed only that man can love and obey a living Spirit; and can be happy in the presence and guidance of a Personal Deity, otherwise than a mollusc, a beetle, or a baboon.

But I will ask the reflective reader to note besides, that it is said to be the use of man to advance God's glory "by his obedience and happiness,"—not by lectures on the Divine wisdom, meant only to show his own. By his obedience, "reasonable," in submission to the Greater Being because He *is* the greater; not because we are as wise as He, and vouchsafe to approve His methods of creation. By our happiness, following on that obedience; not by any happiness snatched or filched out of disobedience; lighting our lives with lightning instead of sunshine—or blackening them with smoke in the day, instead of receiving God's night in its holiness.

Then, lastly, after the crowning of obedience, and fulfilment of joy, comes the joy of Praise,—the "I will magnify Thee, O God my *King*" of the hundred and forty-fifth Psalm;—the "My soul doth magnify the Lord, and my spirit hath rejoiced in God my *Saviour*," of the Magnificat;—the "Bless ye the Lord" of the three

Holy Children;—the "We praise Thee, O Lord" of the Archangels with all the Host of Heaven;—and in the hearts of all, the deepest joy still in the Madonna's thought, For He hath regarded—the lowliness—of His handmaiden,—of His Archangel, or of His first-praying child;—and perfected praise on the lips of the Babe, as on the harp of David.

He hath regarded their *lowliness*. But not—their *vileness*! The horror and shame of the false Evangelical Religion is in its recommending its souls to God, not for their humility, but their sin! Not because they cast their crowns before God's throne, but because they strew His earth with their ashes.

All that is involved in these passionate utterances of my youth was first expanded and then concentrated into the aphorism given twenty years afterwards in my inaugural Oxford lectures, "All great Art is Praise"; and on that aphorism, the yet bolder saying founded, "So far from Art's being immoral, in the ultimate power of it, nothing but Art is moral: Life without Industry is sin, and Industry without Art, brutality" (I forget the words, but that is their purport): and now, in writing beneath the cloudless peace of the snows of Chamouni, what must be the really final words of the book, which their beauty inspired and their strength guided, I am able, with yet happier and calmer heart than ever heretofore, to enforce its simplest assurance of Faith, that the knowledge of what is beautiful leads on, and is the first step, to the knowledge of the things which are lovely and of good report; and that the laws, the life, and the joy of beauty in the material world of God, are as eternal and sacred parts of His creation as, in the world of spirits, virtue; and in the world of angels, praise.

CHAMOUNI,
   Sunday, September 16th, 1888.

ALFRED LORD TENNYSON

I

TIRESIAS AND OTHER POEMS

1885

To E. FITZGERALD

OLD Fitz, who from your suburb grange,
   Where once I tarried for a while,
Glance at the wheeling Orb of change,
   And greet it with a kindly smile;
Whom yet I see as there you sit
   Beneath your sheltering garden-tree,
And while your doves about you flit,
   And plant on shoulder, hand and knee,
Or on your head their rosy feet,
   As if they knew your diet spares
Whatever moved in that full sheet
   Let down to Peter at his prayers;
Who live on milk and meal and grass;
   And once for ten long weeks I tried
Your table of Pythagoras
   And seemed at first "a thing enskied"
(As Shakespeare has it) airy-light
   To float above the ways of men,
Then fell from that half-spiritual height
   Chill'd, till I tasted flesh again
One night when earth was winter-black,
   And all the heavens flash'd in frost;
And on me, half-asleep, came back
   That wholesome heat the blood had lost,
And set me climbing icy capes
   And glaciers, over which there rolled
To meet me long-arm'd vines with grapes
   Of Eshcol hugeness; for the cold

Without, and warmth within me, wrought
    To mould the dream; but none can say
That Lenten fare makes Lenten thought,
    Who reads your golden Eastern lay,
Than which I know no version done
    In English more divinely well;
A planet equal to the sun
    Which cast it, that large infidel
Your Omar; and your Omar drew
    Full-handed plaudits from our best
In modern letters, and from two,
    Old friends outvaluing all the rest,
Two voices heard on earth no more;
    But we old friends are still alive,
And I am nearing seventy-four,
    While you have touched at seventy-five,
And so I send a birthday line
    Of greeting; and my son, who dipt
In some forgotten book of mine
    With sallow scraps of manuscript,
And dating many a year ago,
    Has hit on this, which you will take
My Fitz, and welcome, as I know
    Less for its own than for the sake
Of one recalling gracious times,
    When, in our younger London days,
You found some merit in my rhymes,
    And I more pleasure in your praise.

II

PREFATORY POEM
TO MY BROTHER'S SONNETS

Midnight, June 30th, 1879

I

MIDNIGHT—in no midsummer tune
The breakers lash the shores:
The cuckoo of a joyless June
Is calling out of doors:

And thou hast vanish'd from thine own
To that which looks like rest,
True brother, only to be known
By those who love thee best.

II

Midnight—and joyless June gone by,
And from the deluged park
The cuckoo of a worse July
Is calling thro' the dark:

But thou art silent underground,
And o'er thee streams the rain,
True poet, surely to be found
When Truth is found again.

III

And, now to these unsummered skies
The summer bird is still,
Far off a phantom cuckoo cries
From out a phantom hill;

And thro' this midnight breaks the sun
Of sixty years away,
The light of days when life begun,
The days that seem to-day,

When all my griefs were shared with thee,
As all my hopes were thine—
As all thou wert was one with me,
May all thou art be mine!

C. M. DOUGHTY

TRAVELS IN ARABIA DESERTA

Preface to the Second Edition

1888

Of surpassing interest to those many minds, which seek after philosophic knowledge and instruction, is the Story of the Earth, Her
manifold living creatures, the human generations and Her ancient
rocks.

Briefly, and with such views as these, not worldly aims, a disciple
of the divine Muse of Spenser and Venerable Chaucer; having spent
the best part of ten years of early manhood, sojourning in succession
in most of the Continental countries, and lastly in Syria, and having
wandered through the length and breadth of Palestine, I reached
Egypt and Sinai; where with Beduin guides, I wandered on, through
the most of that vast mountainous labyrinthine solitude of rainless
valleys; with their sand-wind burnished rocks and stones and in
some of them, often strangely scribbled Nabatean cliff-inscriptions
(the names, the saws and salutations of ancient wayfarers). From
thence gone up to Edom, I visited Petra; and at Maan settlement,
which is a few miles beyond, heard of other Petra-like sculptured
cliff-monuments, bearing many inscriptions, at Medáin Sâlih.
(That was a water-station of the Damascus yearly pilgrims' caravan,
in their long desert way to Medina and Mecca; lying some few
days' journey southward from Maan, but difficult to be reached,
at other times, for danger of the wild Beduins.)

Medain Salih, *i.e.* cities of their reputed prophet Salih, so named
by the pilgrims, being the subject of many Koran fables; but more
properly, from antiquity, el-Héjr, (as it yet is in the mouths of
the country nomads,) was at that time not known to Europeans.

What might be those inscriptions? I was unable to learn from
my Arab companions, save that they were not Arabic. Interested
as I was, in all that pertains to Biblical research, I resolved to
accept the hazard of visiting them.

This was only accomplished later, after more than another year's fruitless endeavours; when finding none other means, I had taken the adventure of journeying thither, in the great Damascus caravan.

Arrived at the place, after three weeks' tedious riding, amongst that often clamorous, mixed and in their religion devout pilgrim-multitude; I found Medáin Sâlih to be an old ruinous sand-plain, with sand-rock cliffs; where our encampment was pitched by a great cistern, defended from the interference of Beduins, by a rude-built Turkish fort or KELLA: whence it is the weary pilgrims draw to drink, for themselves and their numerous camels.

Hardly visible in the next cliffs, was some one of the sculptured monuments, which I was come thus far to seek. Upon the Western horizon appeared, (to me of hardly less interest,) the heads evidently by their forms, of some latent or extinct volcanoes.

During those two months which remained till the returning of the pilgrimage, I visited the monuments and carefully impressed their formal superscriptions; which proved to be sepulchral and Nabatean, from a little earlier and a little later than the beginning of our Era: and found and transcribed some few other upon ancient building-stones, at the neighbour desert settlement, el-ALLY, which are Himyaric.

The pilgrims come again, I did not return with them to Syria; but rode with a friendly sheykh of the district Beduins, to live with them awhile in the high desert. I might thus, I hoped, visit the next Arabian uplands and view those vast waterless marches of the nomad Arabs; tent-dwellers, inhabiting, from the beginning, as it were beyond the World.

Unto this new endeavour, I was but slenderly provided; yet did not greatly err, when I trusted my existence, (which could long endure, as in Sinai, with little more than Heaven's sun and air,) amongst an unlettered and reputed lawless tribesfolk, (with whom, however, I had already some more favourable acquaintance;) which amidst a life of never-ending hardship and want, continue to observe a Great Semitic Law, unwritten; namely the ancient Faith of their illimitable empty wastes. I might find moreover, in so doing, to add something to the common fund of Western know-ledge. The name of Engleysy might stand me first in some stead, where known, perchance remotely, by faint hearsay, in some desert settlement. On the other hand, there must needs remain, as friendly Arab voices warned me, that predatory instinct of Beduins beyond their tents; besides the bitterness and blight of a fanatical religion, in every place.

In the adventure thus begun, there passed over me, amongst the thinly scattered, generally hostile and suspicious inhabitants of that Land of wilderness, nearly two long and partly weary years; but not without happy turns, in the not seldom finding, as I went forth, of human fellowship amongst Arabians and even of some very true and helpful friendships; which, from this long distance of years, I vividly recall and shall, whilst life lasts, continue to esteem with grateful mind. The haps that befel me are narrated in these volumes: wherein I have set down, that which I saw with my eyes, and heard with my ears and thought in my heart; neither more or less.

These volumes, published originally by the Cambridge University Press, have been some time out of print. A re-print has been called for; and is reproduced thus, at the suggestion chiefly of my distinguished friend, Colonel T. E. Lawrence, leader with Feysal, Meccan Prince, of the nomad tribesmen; whom they, as might none other at that time, marching from Jidda, the port of Mecca, were able, (composing, as they went, the tribes' long-standing blood feuds and old enmities), to unite with them in victorious arms, against the corrupt Turkish sovereignty in those parts: and who greatly thus serving his Country's cause and her Allies, from the Eastward, amidst the Great War; has in that imperishable enterprise, traversed the same wide region of Desert Arabia.

[I cannot here take leave, without recording my thankful memory of those good men (all are now passed from us), Henry Bradshaw, Librarian at that time of the Cambridge University Library, and W. Wright, University Professor of Arabic: who together with Robertson Smith, also Professor there of Semitic learning; powerfully persuaded the University Press Syndics, to undertake the costly printing and publishing of the MS. of this work.]

September 1920.

W. H. WHITE

THE AUTOBIOGRAPHY OF
MARK RUTHERFORD

Preface to the Second Edition

1888

THE present edition is a reprint of the first, with corrections of several mistakes which had been overlooked.

There is one observation which I may perhaps be permitted to make on re-reading after some years this autobiography. Rutherford, at any rate in his earlier life, was an example of the danger and the folly of cultivating thoughts and reading books to which he was not equal, and which tend to make a man lonely.

It is all very well that remarkable persons should occupy themselves with exalted subjects, which are out of the ordinary road which ordinary humanity treads; but we who are not remarkable make a very great mistake if we have anything to do with them. If we wish to be happy, and have to live with average men and women, as most of us have to live, we must learn to take an interest in the topics which concern average men and women. We think too much of ourselves. We ought not to sacrifice a single moment's pleasure in our attempt to do something which is too big for us, and as a rule, men and women are always attempting what is too big for them. To ninety-nine young men out of a hundred, or perhaps ninety-nine thousand out of a hundred thousand, the wholesome healthy doctrine is, "Don't bother yourselves with what is beyond you; try to lead a sweet, clean, wholesome life, keep yourselves in health above everything, stick to your work, and when your day is done amuse and refresh yourselves." It is not only a duty to ourselves, but it is a duty to others to take this course. Great men do the world much good, but not without some harm, and we have no business to be troubling ourselves with their dreams if we have duties which lie nearer home amongst persons to whom these dreams are incomprehensible. Many a man goes into his study, shuts himself up with his poetry or his psychology, comes out, half understanding what he has read, is miserable because he cannot find anybody with whom he can talk about it, and misses altogether the far more genuine joy which he could have obtained from a game with his children, or listening to what his wife had to tell him about her neighbours.

"Lor, miss, you haven't looked at your new bonnet to-day," said a servant girl to her young mistress.

"No, why should I? I did not want to go out."

"Oh, how can you? why, I get mine out and look at it every night."

She was happy for a whole fortnight with a happiness cheap at a very high price.

That same young mistress was very caustic upon the women who block the pavement outside drapers' shops, but surely she was unjust. They always seem unconscious, to be enjoying themselves intensely and most innocently, more so probably than an audience at a Wagner concert. Many persons with refined minds are apt to depreciate happiness, especially, if it is of "a low type." Broadly speaking, it is the one thing worth having, and low or high, if it does no mischief, is better than the most spiritual misery.

Metaphysics, and theology, including all speculations on the why and the wherefore, optimism, pessimism, freedom, necessity, causality, and so forth, are not only for the most part loss of time, but frequently ruinous. It is no answer to say that these things force themselves upon us, and that to every question we are bound to give or try to give an answer. It is true, although strange, that there are multitudes of burning questions which we must do our best to ignore, to forget their existence; and it is not more strange, after all, than many other facts in this wonderfully mysterious and defective existence of ours. One fourth of life is intelligible, the other three fourths is unintelligible darkness; and our earliest duty is to cultivate the habit of not looking round the corner.

"Go thy way, eat thy bread with joy, and drink thy wine with a merry heart; for God hath already accepted thy works. Let thy garments be always white, and let not thy head lack ointment. Live joyfully with the wife whom thou lovest all the days of the life of thy vanity, which He hath given thee under the sun, all the days of thy vanity; for that is thy portion in life."

R. S.

APPEARANCE AND REALITY

1893

Introduction

THE writer on metaphysics has a great deal against him. Engaged on a subject which more than others demands peace of spirit, even before he enters on the controversies of his own field, he finds himself involved in a sort of warfare. He is confronted by prejudices hostile to his study, and he is tempted to lean upon those prejudices, within him and around him, which seem contrary to the first. It is on the preconceptions adverse to metaphysics in general that I am going to make some remarks by way of introduction. We may agree, perhaps, to understand by metaphysics an attempt to know reality as against mere appearance, or the study of first principles or ultimate truths, or again the effort to comprehend the universe, not simply piecemeal or by fragments, but somehow as a whole. Any such pursuit will encounter a number of objections. It will have to hear that the knowledge which it desires to obtain is impossible altogether; or, if possible in some degree, is yet practically useless; or that, at all events, we can want nothing beyond the old philosophies. And I will say a few words on these arguments in their order.

(a) The man who is ready to prove that metaphysical knowledge is wholly impossible has no right here to any answer. He must be referred for conviction to the body of this treatise. And he can hardly refuse to go there, since he himself has, perhaps unknowingly, entered the arena. He is a brother metaphysician with a rival theory of first principles. And this is so plain that I must excuse myself from dwelling on the point. To say the reality is such that our knowledge cannot reach it, is a claim to know reality; to urge that our knowledge is of a kind which must fail to transcend appearance, itself implies that transcendence. For, if we had no idea of a beyond, we should assuredly not know how to talk about failure or success.   And the test, by which we distinguish them, must obviously be some acquaintance with the nature of the goal. Nay, the would-be sceptic, who presses on us the contradictions of our thoughts, himself asserts dogmatically.   For these contradictions might be ultimate and absolute truth, if the nature of the reality were not known to be otherwise.   But this introduction is not the place to discuss a class of objections which are themselves, however unwillingly, metaphysical views, and which a little acquainance with the subject commonly serves to dispel.   So far as is necessary, they will be dealt with in their proper place; and I will therefore pass to the second main argument against metaphysics.

(b) It would be idle to deny that this possesses great force. "Metaphysical knowledge," it insists, "may be possible theoretically, and even actual, if you please, to a certain degree; but, for all that, it is practically no knowledge worth the name."   And this objection may be rested on various grounds.   I will state some of these, and will make the answers which appear to me to be sufficient.

The first reason for refusing to enter on our field is an appeal to the confusion and barrenness which prevail there.   "The same problems," we hear it often, "the same disputes, the same sheer failure.   Why not abandon it and come out?   Is there nothing else more worth your labour?"   To this I shall reply more fully soon, but will at present deny entirely that the problems have not altered.   The assertion is about as true and about as false as would be a statement that human nature has not changed.   And it seems indefensible when we consider that in history metaphysics has not only been acted on by the general development, but has also reacted.   But apart from historical questions, which are here not in place, I am inclined to take my stand on the admitted possibility. If the object is not impossible, and the adventure suits us—what then?   Others far better than ourselves have wholly failed—so you say.   But the man who succeeds is not apparently always the man of most merit, and even in philosophy's cold world perhaps some fortunes go by favour.   One never knows until one tries.

But to the question, if seriously I expect to succeed, I must, of course, answer, No.   I do not suppose, that is, that satisfactory knowledge is possible.   How much we can ascertain about reality will be discussed in this book; but I may say at once that I expect a very partial satisfaction. I am so bold as to believe that we have a knowledge of the Absolute, certain and real, though I am sure that our comprehension is miserably incomplete. But I dissent emphatically from the conclusion that, because imperfect, it is worthless. And I must suggest to the objector that he should open his eyes and should consider human nature. Is it possible to abstain from thought about the universe? I do not mean merely that to every one the whole body of things must come in the gross, whether consciously or unconsciously, in a certain way. I mean that, by various causes, even the average man is compelled to wonder and to reflect. To him the world, and his share in it, is a natural object of thought, and seems likely to remain one. And so, when poetry, art, and religion have ceased wholly to interest, or when they show no longer any tendency to struggle with ultimate problems and to come to an understanding with them; when the sense of mystery and enchantment no longer draws the mind to wander aimlessly and to love it knows not what; when, in short, twilight has no charm—then metaphysics will be worthless. For the question (as things are now) is not whether we are to reflect and ponder on ultimate truth—for perhaps most of us do that, and are not likely to cease. The question is merely as to the way in which this should be done. And the claim of metaphysics is surely not unreasonable. Metaphysics takes its stand on this side of human nature, this desire to think about and comprehend reality. And it merely asserts that, if the attempt is to be made, it should be done as thoroughly as our nature permits. There is no claim on its part to supersede other functions of the human mind; but it protests that, if we are to think, we should sometimes try to think properly. And the opponent of metaphysics, it appears to me, is driven to a dilemma. He must either condemn all reflection on the essence of things,—and, if so, he breaks, or, rather, tries to break, with part of the highest side of human nature,—or else he allows us to think but not to think strictly. He permits, that is to say, the exercise of thought so long as it is entangled with other functions of our being; but as soon as it attempts a pure development of its own, guided by the principles of its own distinctive working, he prohibits it forth-

of the Divine, or, again, may realize it with an intenser consciousness; but there is no calling or pursuit which is a private road to the Deity. And assuredly the way through speculation upon ultimate truths, though distinct and legitimate, is not superior to others. There is no sin, however prone to it the philosopher may be, which philosophy can justify so little as spiritual pride.

MARY KINGSLEY

TRAVELS IN WEST AFRICA

1897

Preface

To THE READER.—What this book wants is not a simple Preface
but an apology, and a very brilliant and convincing one at that.
Recognising this fully, and feeling quite incompetent to write such
a masterpiece, I have asked several literary friends to write one for
me, but they have kindly but firmly declined, stating that it is
impossible satisfactorily to apologise for my liberties with Lindley
Murray and the Queen's English. I am therefore left to make a
feeble apology for this book myself, and all I can personally say is
that it would have been much worse than it is had it not been for
Dr. Henry Guillemard, who has not edited it, or of course the
whole affair would have been better, but who most kindly has gone
through the proof sheets, lassoing prepositions which were straying
outside their sentence stockade, taking my eye off the water cask
and fixing it on the scenery where I meant it to be, saying firmly
in pencil on margins "No you don't," when I was committing
some more than usually heinous literary crime, and so on. In
cases where his activities in these things may seem to the reader to
have been wanting, I beg to state that they really were not. It is
I who have declined to ascend to a higher level of lucidity and
correctness of diction than I am fitted for. I cannot forbear from
mentioning my gratitude to Mr. George Macmillan for his patience
and kindness with me,—a mere jungle of information on West
Africa. Whether you my reader will share my gratitude is, I fear,
doubtful, for if it had not been for him I should never have attempted
to write a book at all, and in order to excuse his having induced me
to try I beg to state that I have written only on things that I know
from personal experience and very careful observation. I have
never accepted an explanation of a native custom from one person
alone, nor have I set down things as being prevalent customs from

179

having seen a single instance. I have endeavoured to give an honest account of the general state and manner of life in Lower Guinea and some description of the various types of country there. In reading this section you must make some allowance for my love of this sort of country, with its great forests and rivers and its animistic-minded inhabitants, and for my ability to be more comfortable there than in England. Your superior culture-instincts may militate against your enjoying West Africa, but if you go there you will find things as I have said.

W. B. YEATS

POEMS 1899–1905

Preface

I HAVE gathered into this book all the poems I have finished since
I published "The Wind Among the Reeds" nearly seven years ago,
and as I turn over the pages it seems to me very little to have been
so long about.   The writing of them has kept me pretty busy for
all that, because I have had to destroy so many lines that would
have thrown one play or another out of shape.   During these years,
especially during the last three or four, I have been getting some
practical knowledge of the stage in our Irish dramatic movement,
and I have spent a good part of the time shaping and reshaping some
half-dozen plays in prose or verse.   After I had learned to hold an
audience for an act in prose I found that I had everything to learn
over again in verse, for in dramatic prose one has to prepare principally for actions, and for the thoughts or emotions that bring them
about or arise out of them; but in verse one has to do all this and to
follow as well a more subtle sequence of cause and effect, that moves
through vast sentiments and intricate thoughts that accompany
action, but are not necessary to it.   It is not very difficult to construct a fairly vigorous prose play, and then, when one is certain it
will act, as it stands, to decorate it and encumber it with poetry.
But a play of that kind will never move us poetically, because it
does not uncover, as it were, that high, intellectual, delicately
organized soul of men and of an action, that may not speak aloud
if it do not speak in verse.   I am a little disappointed with the
upshot of so many years, but I know that I have been busy with
the Great Work, no lesser thing than that, although it may be the
Athanor has burned too fiercely, or too faintly and fitfully, or that
the *prima materia* has been ill-chosen.

Some of my friends, and it is always for a few friends one writes,
do not understand why I have not been content with lyric writing.
But one can only do what one wants to do, and to me drama—and

I think it has been the same with other writers—has been the search for more of manful energy, more of cheerful acceptance of whatever arises out of the logic of events, and for clean outline, instead of those outlines of lyric poetry that are blurred with desire and vague regret. All art is in the last analysis an endeavour to condense as out of the flying vapour of the world an image of human perfection, and for its own and not for the art's sake, and that is why the labour of the alchemists, who were called artists in their day, is a befitting comparison for all deliberate change of style. We live with images, that is our renunciation, for only the silent sage or saint can make himself into that perfection, turning the life inward at the tongue as though it heard the cry *Secretum meum mihi*; choosing not, as we do, to say all and know nothing, but to know all and to say nothing.

"The Shadowy Waters," "The King's Threshold," and "On Baile's Strand" are not at all as they were when first printed, for they have been rewritten and rewritten until I feel I can do no better with my present subjects and experience. I am the least confident about "The Shadowy Waters," for it is so unlike what it was when last played that it is a new play, and I have but tried it at rehearsal, and without its scenery and its costumes, and that harp which is to burn with a faint fire. It is to be judged, like all my plays, as part of an attempt to create a national dramatic literature in Ireland, and it takes upon itself its true likeness of a Jack-a-Lantern among more natural and simple things, when set among the plays of my fellow-workers. What I have done is but a form and colour in an elaborate composition, where they have painted the other forms and colours. The extravagance, the joyous irony, the far-flying phantasy, the aristocratic gaiety, the resounding and rushing words of the comedy of the countryside, of the folk as we say, is akin to the elevation of poetry, which can but shrink even to the world's edge from the harsh, cunning, traditionless humour of the towns. I write of the tragic stories told over the fire by people who are in the comedies of my friends, and I never see my work played with theirs that I do not feel that my tragedy heightens their comedy and tragi-comedy, and grows itself more moving and intelligible from being mixed into the circumstance of the world

by the circumstantial art of comedy.   Nor is it only the stories and
the country mind that have made us one school, for we have talked
over one another's work so many times, that when a play of mine
comes into my memory I cannot always tell how much even of the
radical structure I may not owe to the writer of "The Lost Saint,"
or of "The Shadow of the Glen," or more than all, to the writer of
"Hyacinth Halvey"; or that I could have written at all in so heady
a mood if I did not know that one or the other were at hand to
throw a bushel of laughter into the common basket.

I have printed the plays and poems in the order of their first
publication, but so far as the actual writing of verse is concerned
"The Shadowy Waters" and "On Baile's Strand" have been so
much rewritten that they are later than "The King's Threshold."
I have put no explanatory notes to the poems and very few to the
plays, for impatient readers do not read even the shortest notes, and
the patient would cry out upon an arid summary, for they can read
the legends in those strange and beautiful books, canonical with
most of us in Ireland now, Lady Gregory's "Gods and Fighting
Men" and "Cuchulain of Muirthemne."

IN THE SEVEN WOODS,
  18 *May*, 1906.

THOMAS HARDY

LATE LYRICS AND EARLIER

1922

Apology

ABOUT half the verses that follow were written quite lately. The rest are older, having been held over in MS. when past volumes were published, on considering that these would contain a sufficient number of pages to offer readers at one time, more especially during the distractions of the war. The unusually far back poems to be found here are, however, but some that were overlooked in gathering previous collections. A freshness in them, now unattainable, seemed to make up for their inexperience and to justify their inclusion. A few are dated; the dates of others are not discoverable.

The launching of a volume of this kind in neo-Georgian days by one who began writing in mid-Victorian, and has published nothing to speak of for some years, may seem to call for a few words of excuse or explanation. Whether or no, readers may feel assured that a new book is submitted to them with great hesitation at so belated a date. Insistent practical reasons, however, among which were requests from some illustrious men of letters who are in sympathy with my productions, the accident that several of the poems have already seen the light, and that dozens of them have been lying about for years, compelled the course adopted, in spite of the natural disinclination of a writer whose works have been so frequently regarded askance by a pragmatic section here and there, to draw attention to them once more.

I do not know that it is necessary to say much on the contents of the book, even in deference to suggestions that will be mentioned presently. I believe that those readers who care for my poems at all—readers to whom no passport is required—will care for this new instalment of them, perhaps the last, as much as for any that have preceded them.   Moreover, in the eyes of a less friendly class the pieces, though a very mixed collection indeed, contain, so far as I am able to see, little or nothing in technic or teaching that can be considered a Star-Chamber matter, or so much as agitating to a ladies' school; even though, to use Wordsworth's observation in his Preface to *Lyrical Ballads*, such readers may suppose "that by the act of writing in verse an author makes a formal engagement that he will gratify certain known habits of association: that he not only thus apprises the reader that certain classes of ideas and expressions will be found in his book, but that others will be carefully excluded."

It is true, nevertheless, that some grave, positive, stark, delineations are interspersed among those of the passive, lighter, and traditional sort presumably nearer to stereotyped tastes.   For— while I am quite aware that a thinker is not expected, and, indeed, is scarcely allowed, now more than heretofore, to state all that crosses his mind concerning existence in this universe, in his attempts to explain or excuse the presence of evil and the incongruity of penalizing the irresponsible—it must be obvious to open intelligences that, without denying the beauty and faithful service of certain venerable cults, such disallowance of "obstinate questionings" and "blank misgivings" tends to a paralysed intellectual stalemate.   Heine observed nearly a hundred years ago that the soul has her eternal rights; that she will not be darkened by statutes, nor lullabied by the music of bells.   And what is to-day, in allusion to the present author's pages, alleged to be "pessimism" is, in truth, only such "questionings" in the exploration of reality, and is the first step towards the soul's betterment, and the body's also.

If I may be forgiven for quoting my own old words, let me repeat what I printed in this relation more than twenty years ago, and wrote much earlier, in a poem entitled "In Tenebris":

If way to the Better there be, it exacts a full look at the Worst:

that is to say, by the exploration of reality, and its frank recognition stage by stage along the survey, with an eye to the best consummation possible: briefly, evolutionary meliorism.   But it is called pessimism nevertheless; under which word, expressed with condemnatory emphasis, it is regarded by many as some pernicious new thing (though so old as to underlie the Gospel scheme, and even to permeate the Greek drama); and the subject is charitably left to decent silence, as if further comment were needless.

Happily there are some who feel such Levitical passing-by to be, alas, by no means a permanent dismissal of the matter; that comment on where the world stands is very much the reverse of needless in these disordered years of our prematurely afflicted century: that amendment and not madness lies that way. And looking down the future these few hold fast to the same: that whether the human and kindred animal races survive till the exhaustion or destruction of the globe, or whether these races perish and are succeeded by others before that conclusion comes, pain to all upon it, tongued or dumb, shall be kept down to a minimum by loving-kindness, operating through scientific knowledge, and actuated by the modicum of free will conjecturally possessed by organic life when the mighty necessitating forces—unconscious or other—that have "the balancings of the clouds," happen to be in equilibrium, which may or may not be often.

To conclude this question I may add that the argument of the so-called optimists is neatly summarized in a stern pronouncement against me by my friend Mr. Frederic Harrison in a late essay of his, in the words: "This view of life is not mine." The solemn declaration does not seem to me to be so annihilating to the said "view" (really a series of fugitive impressions which I have never tried to co-ordinate) as is complacently assumed. Surely it embodies a too human fallacy quite familiar in logic. Next, a knowing reviewer, apparently a Roman Catholic young man, speaks, with some rather gross instances of the *suggestio falsi* in his whole article, of "Mr. Hardy refusing consolation," the "dark gravity of his ideas," and so on. When a Positivist and a Romanist agree there must be something wonderful in it, which should make a poet sit up. But . . . O that 'twere possible!

I would not have alluded in this place or anywhere else to such casual personal criticisms—for casual and unreflecting they must be—but for the satisfaction of two or three friends in whose opinion a short answer was deemed desirable, on account of the continual repetition of these criticisms, or more precisely, quizzings. After all, the serious and truly literary inquiry in this connection is: Should a shaper of such stuff as dreams are made on disregard considerations of what is customary and expected, and apply himself to the real function of poetry, the application of ideas to life (in Matthew Arnold's familiar phrase)? This bears more particularly on what has been called the "philosophy" of these poems—usually reproved as "queer." Whoever the author may be that undertakes such application of ideas in this "philosophic" direction—where it is specially required—glacial judgments must inevitably fall upon him amid opinion whose arbiters largely decry individuality, to whom *ideas* are oddities to smile at, who are moved by a yearning the reverse of that of the Athenian inquirers on Mars Hill; and stiffen their features not only at sound of a new thing, but at a restatement of old things in new terms. Hence should anything of this sort in the following adumbrations seem "queer"—should any of them seem to good Panglossians to embody strange and disrespectful conceptions of this best of all possible worlds, I apologize; but cannot help it.

Such divergences, which, though piquant for the nonce, it would be affectation to say are not saddening and discouraging likewise, may, to be sure, arise sometimes from superficial aspect only, writer and reader seeing the same thing at different angles. But in palpable cases of divergence they arise, as already said, whenever a serious effort is made towards that which the authority I have cited —who would now be called old-fashioned, possibly even parochial —affirmed to be what no good critic could deny as the poet's province, the application of ideas to life. One might shrewdly guess, by the by, that in such recommendation the famous writer may have overlooked the cold-shouldering results upon an enthusiastic disciple that would be pretty certain to follow his putting the high aim in practice, and have forgotten the disconcerting experience of Gil Blas with the Archbishop.

To add a few more words to what has already taken up too many, there is a contingency liable to miscellanies of verse that I have never seen mentioned, so far as I can remember; I mean the chance little shocks that may be caused over a book of various character like the present and its predecessors by the juxtaposition of unrelated, even discordant, effusions; poems perhaps years apart in the making, yet facing each other. An odd result of this has been that dramatic anecdotes of a satirical and humorous intention following verse in graver voice, have been read as misfires because they raise the smile that they were intended to raise, the journalist, deaf to the sudden change of key, being unconscious that he is laughing with the author and not at him. I admit that I did not foresee such contingencies as I ought to have done, and that people might not perceive when the tone altered. But the difficulties of arranging the themes in a graduated kinship of moods would have been so great that irrelation was almost unavoidable with efforts so diverse. I must trust for right note-catching to those finely-touched spirits who can divine without half a whisper, whose intuitiveness is proof against all the accidents of inconsequence. In respect of the less alert, however, should any one's train of thought be thrown out of gear by a consecutive piping of vocal reeds in jarring tonics, without a semiquaver's rest between, and be led thereby to miss the writer's aim and meaning in one out of two contiguous compositions, I shall deeply regret it.

Having at last, I think, finished with the personal points that I was recommended to notice, I will forsake the immediate object of this Preface; and, leaving *Late Lyrics* to whatever fate it deserves, digress for a few moments to more general considerations. The thoughts of any man of letters concerned to keep poetry alive cannot but run uncomfortably on the precarious prospects of English verse at the present day. Verily the hazards and casualties surrounding the birth and setting forth of almost every modern creation in numbers are ominously like those of one of Shelley's paper-boats on a windy lake. And a forward conjecture scarcely permits the hope of a better time, unless men's tendencies should change. So indeed of all art, literature, and "high thinking" nowadays. Whether owing to the barbarizing of taste in the younger minds by the dark madness of the late war, the unabashed cultivation of selfishness in all classes, the plethoric growth of knowledge simultaneously with the stunting of wisdom, "a degrading thirst after outrageous stimulation" (to quote Wordsworth again), or from any other cause, we seem threatened with a new Dark Age.

I formerly thought, like other much exercised writers, that so far as literature was concerned a partial cause might be impotent or mischievous criticism; the satirizing of individuality, the lack of whole-seeing in contemporary estimates of poetry and kindred work, the knowingness affected by junior reviewers, the overgrowth of meticulousness in their peerings for an opinion, as if it were a cultivated habit in them to scrutinize the tool-marks and be blind to the building, to hearken for the key-creaks and be deaf to the diapason, to judge the landscape by a nocturnal exploration with a flash-lantern. In other words, to carry on the old game of sampling the poem or drama by quoting the worst line or worst passage only, in ignorance or not of Coleridge's proof that a versification of any length neither can be nor ought to be all poetry; of reading meanings into a book that its author never dreamt of writing there. I might go on interminably.

But I do not now think any such temporary obstructions to be the cause of the hazard, for these negligences and ignorances, though they may have stifled a few true poets in the run of generations, disperse like stricken leaves before the wind of next week, and are no more heard of again in the region of letters than their writers themselves. No: we may be convinced that something of the deeper sort mentioned must be the cause.

In any event poetry, pure literature in general, religion—I include religion, in its undogmatic sense, because poetry and religion touch each other, or rather modulate into each other; are indeed, often but different names for the same thing—these, I say, the visible signs of mental and emotional life, must like all other things keep moving, becoming; even though at present, when belief in witches of Endor is displacing the Darwinian theory and "the truth that shall make you free," men's minds appear, as above noted, to be moving backwards rather than on. I speak somewhat sweepingly, and should except many thoughtful writers in verse and prose; also men in certain worthy but small bodies of various denominations, and perhaps in the homely quarter where advance might have been the very least expected a few years back—the English Church —if one reads it rightly as showing evidence of "removing those things that are shaken," in accordance with the wise Epistolary recommendation to the Hebrews. For since the historic and once august hierarchy of Rome some generation ago lost its chance of being the religion of the future by doing otherwise, and throwing over the little band of New Catholics who were making a struggle for continuity by applying the principle of evolution to their own faith, joining hands with modern science, and outflanking the hesitating English instinct towards liturgical restatement (a flank march which I at the time quite expected to witness, with the gathering of many millions of waiting agnostics into its fold); since then, one may ask, what other purely English establishment than the Church, of sufficient dignity and footing, with such strength of old association, such scope for transmutability, such architectural spell, is left in this country to keep the shreds of morality together?

It may indeed be a forlorn hope, a mere dream, that of an alliance between religion, which must be retained unless the world is to perish, and complete rationality, which must come, unless also the world is to perish, by means of the interfusing effect of poetry— "the breath and finer spirit of all knowledge; the impassioned expression of science," as it was defined by an English poet who was quite orthodox in his ideas.   But if it be true, as Comte argued, that advance is never in a straight line, but in a looped orbit, we may, in the aforesaid ominous moving backward, be doing it *pour mieux sauter*, drawing back for a spring.   I repeat that I forlornly hope so, notwithstanding the supercilious regard of hope by Schopenhauer, von Hartmann, and other philosophers down to Einstein who have my respect.   But one dares not prophesy.   Physical, chronological, and other contingencies keep me in these days from critical studies and literary circles

> *Where once we held debate, a band*
> *Of youthful friends, on mind and art*

(if one may quote Tennyson in this century [1]).   Hence I cannot know how things are going so well as I used to know them, and the aforesaid limitations must quite prevent my knowing henceforward.

February 1922.

[1] In the first edition Hardy wrote "in this century of free verse," but later dropped the last three words.   There are a few other variants.

PRINTED IN GREAT BRITAIN
BY R. & R. CLARK, LIMITED
EDINBURGH